The Story of SWALLOWFIELD

A SHORT HISTORY OF THE BIGG FAMILY IN WEST SUSSEX AND AUSTRALIA

Tony Turner

Published by A.R. Turner

Typeset by Serco Media & Design
Unit 3 33-35 Woodthorpe Road
Ashford Middlesex TW15 2RP
England

Printed by Yale Press Limited
Delga House
Carmichael Road
Norwood, London SE25 5LY
England

ISBN 0-9540857-0-1

First edition April 2001

Copies available from A.R. Turner
11 Lime Kiln Road
Mannings Heath Horsham
West Sussex RH13 6JH
England

Disclaimer

Whilst every reasonable endeavour has been made to ensure the accuracy of the material in this book, it should be accepted that memories are dimmed by time, and the period covered by this research reaches back over 150 years. No liability will be accepted for any inadvertent inaccuracies, or consequences stemming therefrom. Nevertheless, the author would be pleased to have any inaccuracies brought to his attention.

They shut the way through the woods
Seventy years ago.
Weather and rain have undone it again,
And now you would never know
There was once a way through the woods
Before they planted the trees.
It is underneath the coppice and heath,
And the thin anemones.
Only the keeper sees
That, where the ring-dove broods,
And the badgers roll at ease,
There was once a way through the woods.

'The Way Through the Woods'
Rudyard Kipling 1865-1936

This book is dedicated to the memory of
Warwick Curtis

Map showing the locations of Swallowfield, The Hyde and St. Andrew's church, Nuthurst

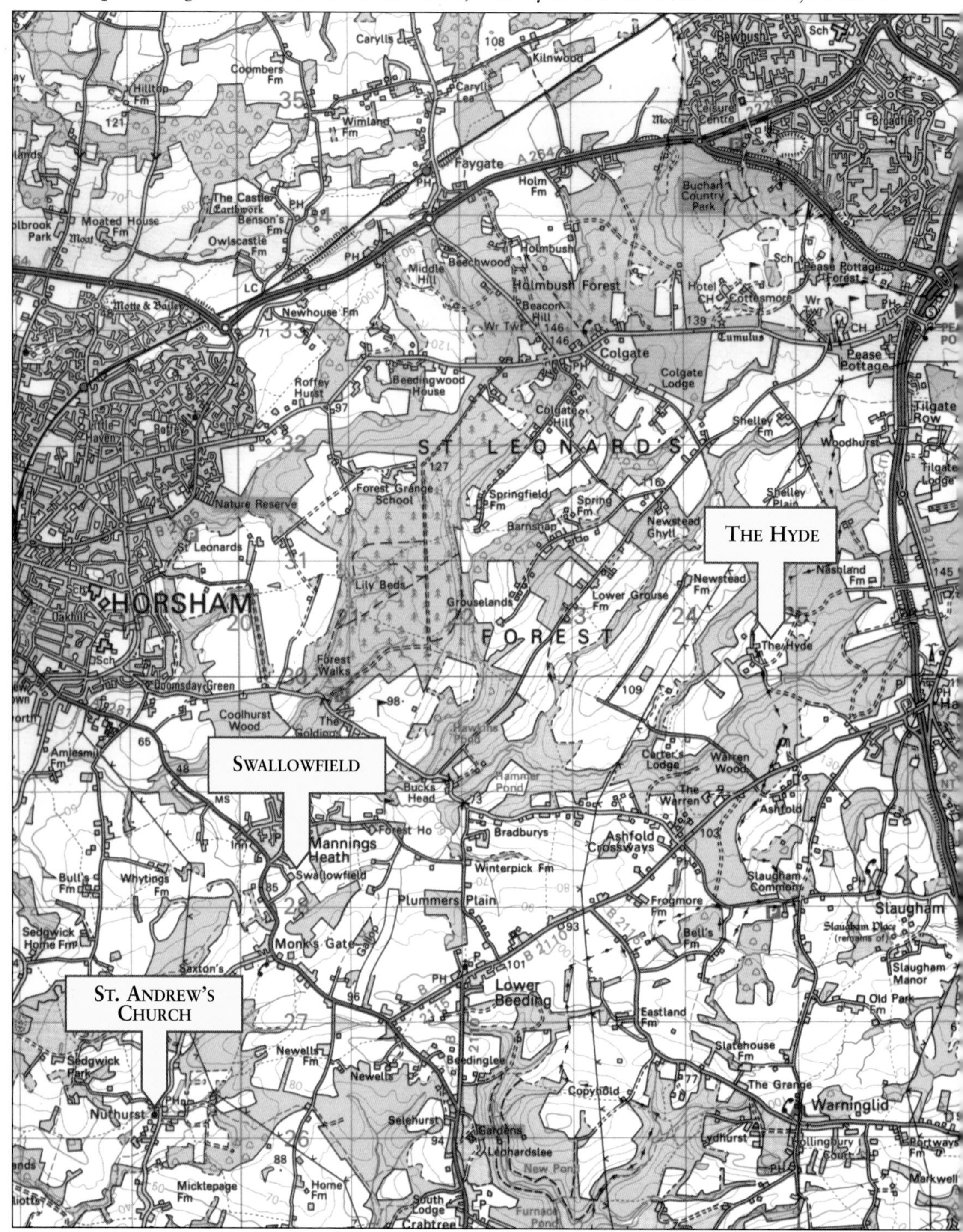

FOREWORD

This is the story of the Bigg family and their fine estate at Mannings Heath in West Sussex. Sadly, the Bigg family are no longer owners of Swallowfield, and the old house and grounds have lacked care and attention in recent times. But the wheel has turned full circle and today the property is undergoing careful and extensive restoration and renovation in the hands of the new owner, Ian Waite. Ian's aim is to bring Swallowfield back to its old glory, not necessarily in exactly its early form in the days of Smith Henry and Augusta Bigg, but extended in sympathy with their original vision.

The origins of this book go back to Saturday 14th June 1997 when, after a wedding service in St. Andrew's Church, in the Parish of Nuthurst, West Sussex, two people wandered into the church and looked as if they needed some help. Speaking to them they said they were interested in finding the graves of some long since departed relatives, the Bigg family. At that time all I knew about the Biggs was that they had lived at the large local estate called Swallowfield and that there was a memorial window to Smith Henry and Augusta Bigg in the Church of the Good Shepherd at Mannings Heath, a few miles away from Nuthurst. So, I took the couple, John and Judith Fitz-Henry, who were from Sydney, Australia to Mannings Heath and showed them the stained-glass windows and the entrance to the Swallowfield estate, closed and derelict so far as I knew.

And that was the start of my learning about Swallowfield, the Bigg family and their offspring, the connections with Australia and what the future holds for the old estate.

The Fitz-Henrys introduced me to Pat, wife of the late Warwick Curtis, whose Bigg/Curtis research had opened the door to an amazing amount of information. Pat and others of 'the clan', in England, Australia and New Zealand, had conducted years of patient, long-distance research into the family's history, and this was made available to me and forms the content of Chapters 1 to 7, as well as Chapters 11 and 12. So without the contributions of all these good folk none of this would have been possible. I acknowledge with grateful thanks the vast amount of material provided to me by Pat Curtis, Judith Fitz-Henry, Nancy McLean, Keith Bigg and the family of Cecil Delmar Curtis.

As I was then (in early 1998) about to visit New Zealand and Australia, I undertook to make a home video to take out to show Pat and her husband Warwick in Napier, New Zealand and John and Judith Fitz-Henry in Sydney, Australia. It was seen subsequently by Nancy and Keith and others of Bigg descent in Armidale, NSW. Through the video I was able to bring to life for them the places and sights they had largely only visualised in their mind's eye, and from still photos.

The video took in the three churches that feature so prominently in the book; the graves of the Bigg family at Nuthurst; the stained-glass windows at the Good Shepherd and at Slaugham; the Hyde estate, and, of course, the estate and house at Swallowfield. Through the good offices of Ian Waite I was given access to the house and its surrounding parkland and given a full tour of the building works that are now under way to restore the old house. I also talked to Allen Flint about his days in service at Swallowfield in the early 1930s. This gave me a valuable insight into life at Swallowfield in the days of Frederick and Rose Bigg. And Alan's memory for detail, so sharp at the age of 87, provided many surprises and helped solve a lot of hitherto unanswered questions.

By another stroke of good fortune I was able to film an interview with Mary Long, a Churchwarden at St. Mary's, Slaugham, who then told me the history of The Hyde, and what had transpired in recent times. This led in turn to my meeting Mary Habershon at The Hyde.

By another chance I came across the firm of Thomas Eggar Church Adams and their connections with the Bigg family. To all these people I am very grateful, for without their inputs and recollections there would not be a story to tell. I thank them most sincerely.

Throughout 1998 and 1999 more and more information came to light and what was planned at the outset to be a brief booklet has grown into something much more substantial. Much of this has been due to my being given access to the diary of Augusta Bigg, wife of Smith Henry Bigg, or to be more precise, to her diary for the year 1845. This was a key year as at that time the Bigg family was having Swallowfield built for them to occupy. Augusta was a conscientious and careful diarist. She recorded events, conversation and her thoughts in detail, day by day, so what the reader finds in Chapter 2 is a factual account. I have deliberately sought to avoid embellishment, and where a surmise has been made, it should be readily evident.

The most rewarding thing for me has been to capture the story of life and events at Swallowfield before the mists of time drift over them and they are forever lost to future generations. Now we have a glimpse of Swallowfield (and The Hyde at Handcross) past and present; hopefully others in due course will continue the story. There is more that needs to be published. There are several other diaries of Augusta to be transcribed, and the work that is presently being done to renovate Swallowfield also needs to be recorded.

At the time of writing pressure is on the West Sussex authorities to build thousands of new homes. Horsham and its environs appear to be a prime target for a very high proportion of them. Pray God that this lovely piece of old historic Sussex does not get overtaken by the developers, and that in a hundred years from now the stands of oaks, the woodlands, the pasture and the imposing Victorian mansion on the ridge will still be there.

So, this is the story of the Bigg family and of their fine house, which still stands today in its beautiful position on a Sussex ridge looking south towards the sea. It is a simple tale, but one which tells how a strong and continuing link has been created between the original Swallowfield in Mannings Heath and a distant Swallowfield situated thousands of miles away on the other side of the world, at Armidale in New South Wales, Australia.

Because it spans several generations of a family's history it contains a rich and fascinating spectrum of events. At one end of the emotional see-saw there is wealth and comfort, whilst at the other we find hardship, tragedy and sorrow. In between are anecdotes that will stir memories and bring a smile to the lips.

I hope you find this walk into the past as enjoyable as I have done.

Tony Turner

Mannings Heath, April 2001

'Swallowfield - open land on the rushing stream'

PART ONE

Edward and Sarah Bigg and their Family

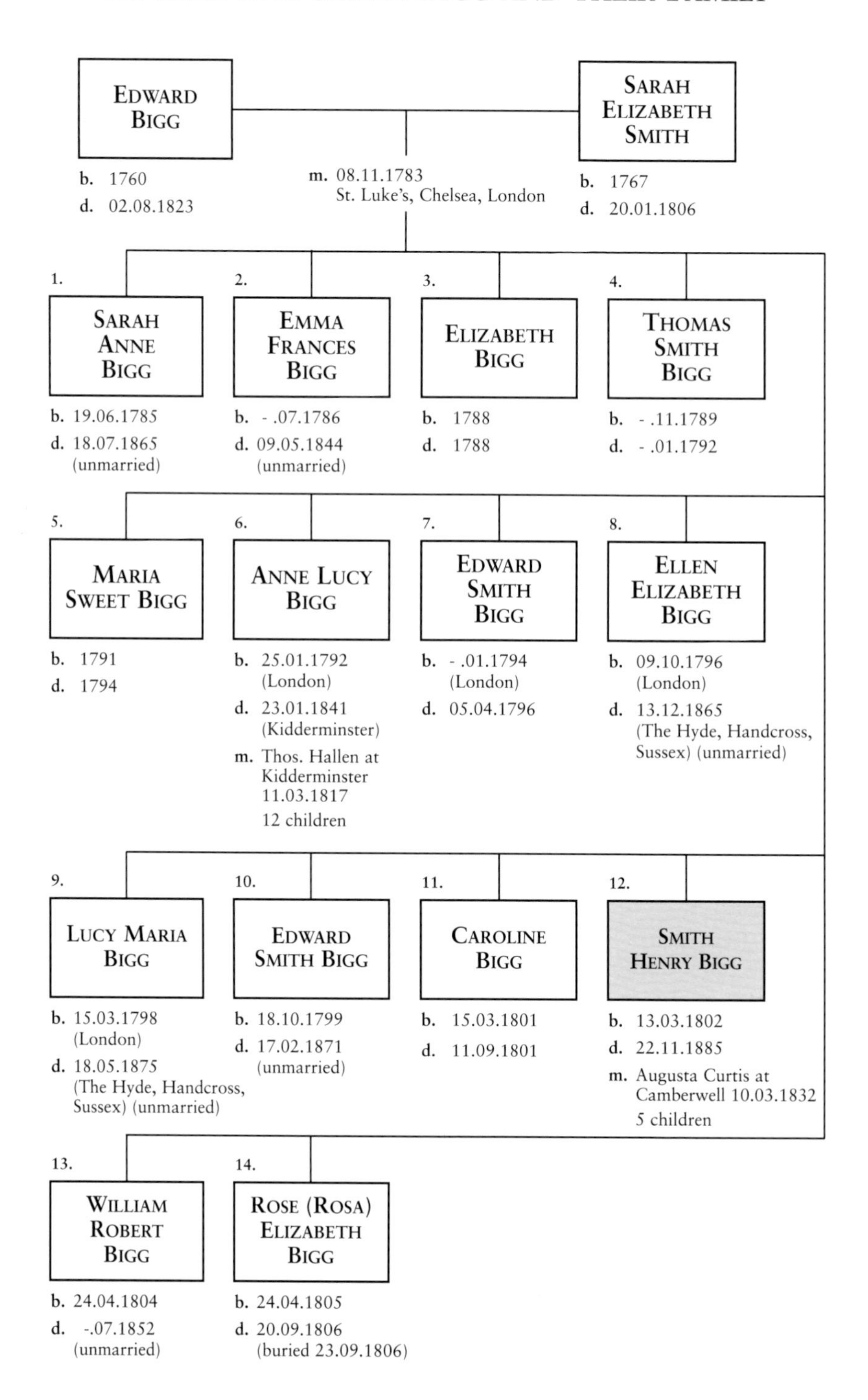

Chart 1

CHAPTER ONE
SMITH HENRY AND AUGUSTA BIGG

The first part of our story about Swallowfield features two key characters, Smith Henry Bigg and his wife Augusta Bigg, and begins in 1845. This immediately poses several questions. Why start with these particular members of the Bigg family? Who were Smith Henry and Augusta, and how did he come to have such an odd christian name? And why start at 1845? The answers to these questions will help set the scene for our story.

WHO WERE SMITH HENRY BIGG AND AUGUSTA BIGG?

Smith Henry Bigg was one of a large family raised by Edward Bigg and Sarah Elizabeth Bigg. (see Chart 1 opposite) His father, Edward, was born in 1760 and his mother seven years later. Edward and Sarah were married on the 8th November 1783 at the Parish Church of St. Luke, Chelsea, Edward being 23 and his bride probably only 16.

The world into which Smith Henry's parents were raised was one that had not long seen the end of perhaps the first truly global conflict, the Seven Years War between England and France. Unlike all previous wars over the centuries the battles of this war had been fought out on nearly every continent and ocean, and when the dust settled with the signing of the Treaty of Paris in 1763, Canada was a British colony rather than a French possession, and the British Empire's grip on India had been immeasurably strengthened. Great Britain was now the most powerful force in the Caribbean. New powers were emerging in Europe and in the New World America's rise had begun.

Whilst the American War of Independence was being fought out, Captain Cook had been exploring the coasts of New Zealand and the east coast of Australia. In the same year that Edward Bigg and Sarah Smith were married (1783) the colonies of America eventually gained their independence. The loss of the former American colonies gave Great Britain impetus to claim new lands in the Pacific, ahead of the French, and thus it was on 13th May 1787 the First Fleet sailed from Portsmouth for Botany Bay. It would not have occurred to Sarah and Edward, as they tended their first two baby girls back home in England, that one day they would have a grandson who would become a pioneer in New South Wales, Australia, and be the one to carry on their family name in this new land.

Smith Henry's parents were a London family living in the Edmonton area of the capital. Several tombstones in the churchyard at Edmonton bear witness to the existence of the Bigg family in the district at this time. His father Edward Bigg rose to become Undersheriff of London in 1810, a not unimportant position and one which would have reflected a sound financial standing.

Edward and Sarah's was a fruitful marriage by any reckoning, with records existing of 14 children, although some of their offspring died very early, as was only too often the case in these times. Elizabeth, Thomas, Maria, Edward, Caroline and Rose (or Rosa) all died before they reached four years of age.

(Large families were then the order of the day, given survival of the children. Anne Stuart was only 37 when she succeeded to the thrones of England, Scotland and Ireland in 1702, but she had already had seventeen pregnancies, and none of her offspring had survived. Physically and mentally debilitated by this continuing round and weakened by the futility of it all, she was an old woman by this time in her life and had to be carried to her coronation in a sedan chair).

By the time Smith Henry was born at the family home in Edmonton on 13th March 1802, the twelfth child born to his mother in 19 years of marriage, he had five surviving older sisters and one brother. Only one further child, William who was born in 1804, survived infancy. These eight children all lived and grew up together as a large family unit, in London, with their wealthy parents.

Sarah, the mother of this large family, died a painful death following *'mortification of the thumb'* as a result of a domestic accident in January 1806, when she cut herself while *'trussing a high pheasant'*. This tragedy occurred when Smith Henry was only three years old. One might ask why a mother of such a well-to-do family was herself engaged in such a domestic culinary chore, when there were servants employed to support them, but that question will have to remain unanswered. It must have been a very painful death and a dreadful loss to Edward and the children.

So, at the age of 46 his father was left with a family of 9 children to raise. However, the eldest child Sarah Anne was 20 at this time and her sister Emma Frances 19, so no doubt they provided their father with much valuable support.

Many of these children of Edward and Sarah will not appear again in our narrative, but there are a number who will, including Sarah Ann, Ellen Elizabeth, Lucy Maria, William Robert, and particularly the eldest brother, Edward Smith.

Smith Henry Bigg.

WHY SMITH HENRY?

Another question we have yet to answer is the reason why "Smith Henry" was so named. The answer would appear to lie with his mother, whose maiden name was Smith. Of the five sons to the marriage of Edward and Sarah, four had Smith incorporated into their Christian names; Thomas Smith Bigg who died aged 2, Edward Smith Bigg who also died at the age of 2, a subsequent Edward (Smith), then our main character Smith Henry. (Why he was called Smith Henry rather than the other way around we will never know, but as we shall see a lot of things went wrong in Smith Henry's lifetime, and maybe the misfortunes started as early as with his naming.) Incidentally, Smith Henry was always referred to as Henry in his lifetime; he has been called Smith Henry throughout this book by the author simply as an expedient to try and distinguish him from the several other Henrys that we come across.

Augusta Bigg, writer of the diaries and wife of Smith Henry.

WHY START OUR STORY WITH SMITH HENRY AND HIS WIFE AUGUSTA?

It was Smith Henry who commissioned the construction of a large new house on the Swallowfield estate on the outskirts of the West Sussex town of Horsham. As far as is known, there was no connection between the Bigg family and Swallowfield before Smith Henry bought the estate. So, it is fitting to begin this story of Swallowfield with the man who had it built and who lived there with his wife and family.

His wife Augusta was a daughter of John Curtis, a prominent stationer and merchant of the city of London. Augusta had been born in 1809 at Ludgate Hill, London, and baptised at St. Bride's Church, Fleet Street, London. They were married on 10th March 1832, probably at St. Giles' Church, Camberwell, London.

WHY START IN 1845?

There are two reasons for starting our tale in this particular year. First, it was the year that the construction of Smith Henry's new house in Mannings Heath was finished and he and his family occupied it. Secondly, we have access to Augusta Bigg's complete diary for that very year. It is a remarkable diary in many respects. She wrote an entry for virtually every day of the year, and not just a brief note about the weather either - although she is so very thorough we could almost work out a weather picture for every day of the year.

In this diary she provides a comprehensive commentary on the daily events of herself and her family. In so doing, she describes the environment and the society she lived in. More than that, Augusta writes of political matters, as well as domestic affairs. We are given an insight into the family's financial situation, and the difficulties of living without all the utilities and inventions that we take for granted in our lives. It is a contemporaneous social history of life in West Sussex in the middle of the nineteenth century.

Although Augusta no doubt kept this personal diary for her private use and never intended that it should be made public, she was so thorough and meticulous that it almost suggests she half expected that others of a later generation might read it. The *'others'* were probably meant to be her descendants, but as this book is primarily a family history, it is hoped she will forgive us for publishing extracts. Where extracts have been used they have been copied exactly from her manuscript, which will account for the almost complete absence of punctuation! If Augusta spoke as she wrote, some of her sentences would have been quite lengthy.

With the aid of that diary we can transport ourselves back to the world of 1845, and that is where the next chapter will take us. So, read on and in the next chapter step back over a hundred and fifty years to follow Smith Henry and his family in 1845, and as you do so remember that what you read actually happened, because Augusta recorded it for us.

Smith Henry and Augusta Bigg and their Family

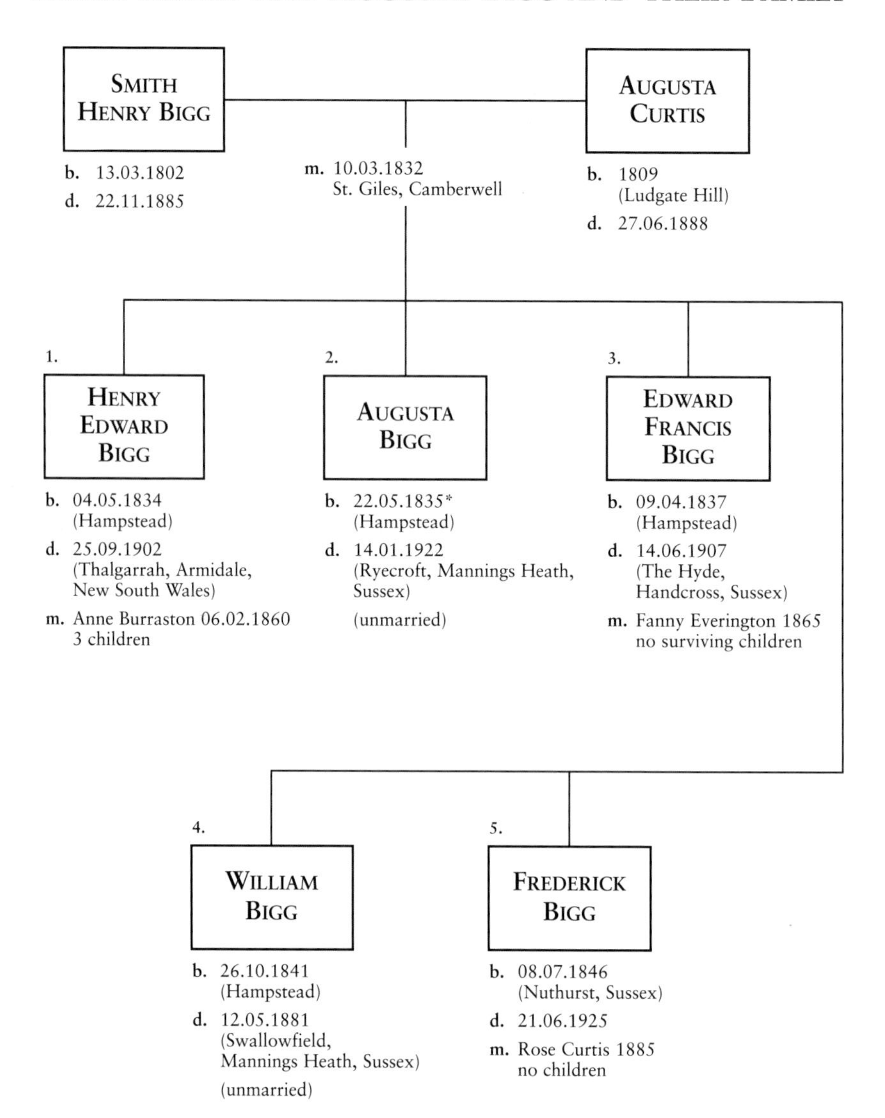

*Family tree sourced

CHAPTER TWO
1845 - A NEW BEGINNING

Smith Henry Bigg stood back from the edge of the platform at Three Bridges station and turned his head aside as the six-wheeled gleaming locomotive hissed and swayed its way slowly past him and lurched to a halt in a huge white cloud of steam. Although he disliked the noise and grime of the new railway, or 'railroad' as his wife would insist on calling it, he had a deep respect for its practicality. Of course the seating lacked the sprung comfort of a carriage and four, but for speed and directness it was quite simply a revelation. To be able to sit back and be carried to London Bridge inside an hour, without the interminable stopping and starting involved with a long road journey, with no horses straining up each gradient as they battled to find their breath and keep their footing over the rough surface, was truly a godsend. To be able to travel without the teeming mayhem that would be encountered as the poor country roads gave way to the slow-moving traffic of wagons, omnibuses, chaises, coaches and humanity on the approaches to the metropolis, was still something that left him thankful.

Stepping into the smartly varnished carriage with his three companions, he nodded deferentially to his fellow passengers, and settled himself with his back to the locomotive. Experience had taught him that the predominance of the soot, sparks and coal dust that was thrown out of the tall chimney of the engine fell on to the forward-facing passengers, but even so, he sat on his cape to protect his clothes and covered his black silk hat as best he could. Still, it was better travelling like this, in First Class, he thought, at least we have a roof over our heads, whereas the poor souls travelling Third Class would be exposed to the elements, as well as the grime.[1]

The weather that day was promising with little threat of the showers of the previous few days. The five mile drive from the house they were renting at Horsham to the station in the omnibus had been quite enjoyable.

But Smith Henry's mind turned to the business of the day, and thoughts of the pleasant fields and woods they had trotted through an hour earlier quickly slipped from his mind. Success today was important. No, he couldn't allow himself to describe it as being vital, but it was a serious matter nonetheless. He was going to see Mr Veal to arrange for a loan - funds to bridge their present difficulty, capital to pay for the continuing expenditure on the building of their new home, Swallowfield.

That it should come to this, he mused. That he should need to borrow money when, only a little over a year ago, he would have described his situation as almost wealthy, rather than just comfortable. And then the mistake had been made which had changed their circumstances, setting them back for some years, it would seem. Their 'imprudence', as Augusta chose to describe it. Dear Augusta, she would never reproach him for what had happened, but she had been disturbed by their situation, he could tell. Now here they were, embarked on a course to move their home from West End, near

1. *Third class carriages were colloquially known as 'rubbish carts'.*

Hampstead on the outskirts of London to Mannings Heath, a few miles south of Horsham in West Sussex, to live in a fine house that was being built for them - with a shortfall in working capital! Smith Henry had real concern that the financial difficulty presently affecting their lives would not easily be solved. True, he reasoned to himself, at the age of 43 as a respected employee of the East India Company in the capital, and with the first few months of the year of our Lord 1845 suggesting a time of continuing prosperity for the country, he should soon be able to position himself to better advantage financially. But he was a worrier by nature, and the nagging doubts persisted. Things would be easier if he could sell his other property, a farm at Willesden.

That had always been part of the plan, but the Willesden farm hadn't been sold yet and the money it was to have generated was sorely needed.

Having bought the 84 acre estate at Swallowfield, the building work on the new house was now draining away his funds faster than he had expected, and this would be likely to continue for the next few months until it was ready for him, Augusta and the children to move in to.

Smith Henry sighed. His brother Edward was the lucky one. He had inherited a hunting lodge and a large estate near Handcross (a small village not far away from Horsham) four years earlier, with a sizeable parcel of land into the bargain. He had re-built the main house in a grand style on his property without any financial hardship. Perhaps this had tempted him to try and emulate Edward's boldness.

For the time being he and Augusta were living in a property they had rented from Mrs Dunbar on the outskirts of Horsham, so that he could take advantage of the new railway line at Three Bridges to get to Town, and from where he would be close enough to Mannings Heath to keep a watching eye over the work at Swallowfield. It was a convenient place to live for Augusta and the children, and the servants of the household for that matter, since Horsham town centre was a short distance away and within easy walking distance. The idea of moving close to the new home while it was being prepared was a recognised step these days, and his friends and colleagues thought it a sensible and prudent arrangement.

Being close to Edward's fine estate at Handcross, a little over two miles away to the east, was another advantage. Regular visits to Edward and his other unmarried brothers and sisters at The Hyde at Handcross were a blessed relief for him and the family. The upheaval they were experiencing in making the move of their household to West Sussex was in part assuaged by the warmth of the welcome they were always assured of receiving at The Hyde. Large, spacious, set in over 900 acres of woodlands, forest, agricultural land, lakes and wonderful gardens, it represented a haven for them, a place of permanence and solitude in a sea of change.

The children, of course, knew nothing of the difficult financial situation being addressed by their father. To them, life was one great adventure as they settled down in their new surroundings. Being born and brought up in London, they had always relished coming down to see Uncle Edward and his sisters Ellen and Lucy and his brother William at The Hyde, and having the opportunity to run and play to their hearts' content on the estate. The family had all stayed with Edward and the family at

The Hyde over Christmas. Soon they were going to live in the country themselves, have their own fields, woods and a lake to enjoy, and to be within driving distance of their favourite Uncle.

Born in 1834, Henry Edward (Smith Henry's eldest son) was 11, just a year older than his sister Augusta. Edward Francis had come along next and was 8 years old, but little William was only coming up to his fourth birthday. It would do Henry a lot of good to live in the country air; his chest was always a problem and his mother was continually worrying about him, despairing that he would stay fit and well for a period of months. Still, Smith Henry thought, the children would be happy in their new home in the country. But a sudden jolt in the passage of the train broke his musing - and with that his mind instantly returned to his own problems.

Would Veal be there this time when he called to see him? Last time he had come up to London expressly for the purpose of proposing an advancement of funds, Veal had been absent and the business was not progressed. How annoying.

And that reminded him of another thing that was bothering him every day - the large chimney of the existing house at Swallowfield. He shouldn't have had it dismantled. Why had he allowed himself to be persuaded to take it down?

As he settled once again into a more comfortable position on the seat of the carriage, he told himself to take a more philosophical view of things. Augusta was forever reassuring him that when the house was finished it would be splendid. He had decided to build his fine new home of local sandstone on the site of the old house called Swallowfield at Mannings Heath, two and a half miles to the south of Horsham in Sussex. The site of the original house had been carefully selected in its own time for good reason. The property had a splendid aspect, situated on a low ridge adjacent to the main stagecoach route from Horsham to Brighton, looking across acres of fields and ancient oak woods, with a distant view of the chalk downlands that heralded the Channel at Shoreham.

There had been a house on this spot since 1574, and the Swallowfield estate of 1743 was reputed to have been some 80 acres. Now this estate was to be the new home for the Bigg family.

Much as he appreciated London, Smith Henry saw this as an opportunity to get out of regular employment and to earn a good living off the land. Added to that, he knew that Augusta and the children needed the fresh air and open space of the country, and what better place to raise a family than at Swallowfield. The Bigg family had arrived in Sussex!

Smith Henry's companions on that train journey to London on the 14th July 1845 were his brothers, Edward (he with the large estate called the Hyde) and William Bigg, as well as a Mr Coverdale and a Mr Hobson, whose affairs also took them to Town that day. They travelled to London from Three Bridges station because it was the only railway line in the south east at that time. Three Bridges was on the newly-constructed London to Brighton line built in 1841 and operated by the London & Brighton Railway Company, with its shining bright green livery. A branch line from Three Bridges to Horsham and on to Portsmouth had been proposed by a Mr Thompson, but had been rejected in January of that year by the Board of Trade. However, by April the decision had been overturned and it was announced in April 1845 that the line would be built. A service from Horsham would be a great benefit to Smith Henry, but his brothers and sisters and their families at the Hyde would continue to use Three Bridges as it was closer for them.[2]

As it transpired, Smith Henry did not borrow money from Mr Veal that day. By the time he returned home later that evening he was able to tell Augusta that brother Edward had again come to their assistance. When they had suffered the setback in their financial position the previous year Edward had been kind enough to advance them a loan, which they were repaying in agreed instalments. In conversation with Edward in London he (Edward) had enquired about their present circumstances and been told the purpose of Smith Henry's journey to Town.

The upshot had been that Edward had offered to suspend future repayments for a period in order that Smith Henry might use the money to fund their expenditure on the work at Swallowfield. This generous offer had been gratefully accepted, but it pained Smith Henry and Augusta to find themselves in such a situation.

Privately, Augusta believed her husband had been too ambitious from the outset in his grand plan to follow his brother to Sussex. It was all very well for Edward to spend large sums in refurbishing his own country estate. After all, as the eldest son of his father (Edward Bigg) he had inherited a considerable sum in 1823 (as well as The Hyde) and could afford to make the commitment. Edward was unmarried and had a profession that provided him with a high income. Edward was a Solicitor and a Justice of the Peace, working from Southampton Buildings in Chancery Lane. In the 1820s he had started a practice in the Horsham area. For the best part of three years Smith Henry had watched his brother improve and furnish The Hyde, as the country estate at Handcross was called. And in the end he had succumbed to the temptation to sell up his own farm and to move his family to a Sussex estate too. But both Augusta and he now knew only too well that they had over-stretched themselves. Their farm at Willesden was still unsold, so their funds were tied up and unavailable to them for the immediate future. They were now seriously embarrassed for cash and were beholden to Edward for support. They knew they had no option but to carry on with the move. There was no going back. To stop work on Swallowfield and to return to West End was unthinkable, and would involve a loss of face that Smith Henry and Augusta would have found unacceptable.

With Smith Henry having to travel to Town regularly to conduct his business, it was left to Augusta to watch over the building works at Swallowfield and, of course, to manage the household and to raise her young family. These were duties that Augusta attended to diligently, as was her way. Work on the house had been going on for several

2. *The first service operated by the B&SCR ran from Croydon to Haywards Heath on 12th July 1841. When the station was built at Three Bridges it was originally called East Crawley. The first train from Brighton to London left Brighton at 6.45 am on 21st September 1841; starting back from London at 9.45am, pulling 13 carriages, it arrived at Brighton 2 hours later. On Easter Monday 1844 the first excursion train on the line, drawn by 4 engines, left London Bridge at 9.00am pulling 45 carriages. More carriages and engines were added along the route and the train drew into Brighton at 1.30pm. The normal time for the journey was 90 minutes for a First Class train, 2 hours for mixed First and Second Class trains, and 2 hours for all-class services. The link from Three Bridges to Horsham was established in 1848.*

months already, and it would be September before the family could expect to move in. The work was extensive because Smith Henry had decided from the outset to take down the existing buildings and to start from the ground up with a new construction. Since the day that decision had been made it had caused her husband a great deal of anguish. All through the first half of that year he had been expressing his doubts about it. At first his anxiety had stemmed from his concern that the existing building had much character that would be forever lost - especially those fine chimneys he was always going on about. Later, as the extent of the work increased and the bills mounted, his worry was compounded by the realisation that he had been imprudent in making such a bold decision. But by the time July had come, even despite the money worries, his mood had changed and he came to accept that once the house was finished, it would be a fine home for them all.

The winter of 1844/5 had been a hard one, with plenty of snow, driving rain and cold winds. It was an unfortunate time to be engaged house-building and progress had been dreadfully slow. As the early spring arrived, the foundations had been completed and by mid-March the flooring boards had arrived. The pace of work thankfully quickened, and by the end of March the upper floor and the bedrooms had taken shape.

On the 27th of that month Augusta had been able to visit her bedroom for the first time, which had just received its first coat of plaster. Unfortunately, Augusta's enthusiasm at seeing the room was tempered by her husband having yet another bout of depression about pulling the old house down, and making himself quite miserable. Within the next few days three rooms had been plastered and the well had been dug.

But again Smith Henry expressed his regrets about what they were doing, and although Augusta tried to placate him, he assured her that he would never get over it. Things were not helped that day by a visiting relative's remark to the effect that the position of the new house was too exposed.

By April 7th Augusta could see that the upstairs rooms had been plastered and the passages laid. The laying of the upstairs floor had begun and the workmen were getting into the drawing room. Outside the new well was 21 feet (7 metres) deep with about 2 feet of water at the bottom. Smith Henry's gloom continued and he now told Augusta he was certain he should never be happy there. Augusta's reaction was to tell him not to be so miserable, which is understandable. A week later Smith Henry was dissatisfied with one of the workmen, whom he suspected of pilfering some potatoes and also removing a slab of oak. The next day the individual concerned, by the name of Dombrok, was discharged and Dinnage appointed to look after things for the present.

There were then two members of the Dinnage family working to prepare Swallowfield for the Bigg family at this time, as Mrs Dinnage was already employed. On 30th May Augusta went to Swallowfield to pay the men and saw that the combined efforts of the Dinnages had much improved the garden. The staircase window had been put in and the last coat of plaster was going up on the back passage and dining room.

Later in the week Augusta ventured up the ladder to see the upstairs rooms and thought them very convenient and comfortable. She also set her mind on having a room made in the roof. The early weeks of June brought the warm weather and Augusta pressed for work to proceed with all haste. On the 9th June the kitchen floor was being paved. It was not all work, however, and there was time for some enjoyment. With the spell of good weather continuing, Augusta went to Swallowfield on the following Thursday morning with young Henry, and they were joined by the rest of the family and the servants in the afternoon. The servants, Nurse and Cook, contrived to have their tea there, with the help of Mrs Dinnage, sitting on the carpenter's bench in the storeroom.

By the end of August the inside doors were hung, the washhouse started and more chimneys erected. On September 20th Augusta's mother decided to come and see the new house that her daughter and her family were about to move into. Thankfully she was pleased with the house in general, but quite horrified to see it so unfinished. With only a week to go before the big day there was not a grate in the house apart from the kitchen range, no WC fitted, not one outer door hung, no banisters and no windows to the rear aspect!

Four days later packing started and the first load of furniture was despatched to Swallowfield. On Friday 26th September 1845 Nurse and three of the children went off to The Hyde to stay for a while until the new house could be made a little more comfortable for them before they moved in.

Two further advance loads of furniture were sent to Swallowfield and Augusta and Caroline Tullett, one of the servants she had recently hired to replace Esther, went along to unpack them.

Augusta was faced with dust and dirt the like of which she had never seen before, and very little comfort. But nothing daunted, she set about making the most of what she found. The full move took place the following day, Saturday. Unfortunately it was a drizzly day, but luckily the furniture did not get very wet. Mr Fuller supplied his covered sprung cart, which took the bedding, piano and dining room furniture. The Fullers' cart did a double run, as did the Biggs' own cart. Before the last load was despatched, Augusta left to walk to her future home, in the wind and rain, only to find the house looked as desolate and miserable as could be imagined. Inside the furniture and effects were spread anywhere and everywhere throughout the house and all the dirt and mud had been walked in. In the kitchen and washhouse there were no windows still and only temporary doors. She immediately sent for Mrs Dinnage to come and help and they made a start as best they could. Rebecca the other servant did not arrive until it was quite dark and before this Augusta had the kitchen swept out and the kitchen window fitted. Smith Henry put up the spare bed while the carpenters put up the beds for the servants. So the night passed safely with Augusta and the other ladies of the household rather afraid of thieves, there being no means of keeping the place secure with no outside doors!

The following day being Sunday Augusta would normally have gone to church (at least once, more probably twice.) Today, however, everything conspired to go wrong. The dreadful confusion and mess they were in simply made it essential that they get on with the unpacking and clearing up. Smith Henry was particularly set on getting to work. On top of that, a chest of drawers with some of Augusta's clothing had been left behind, so she felt she had not got appropriate clothes to wear. And to add to the situation it still continued to rain. Not only did Augusta put off her churchgoing, she also declined Miss Bigg's invitation to go over to The Hyde in the afternoon.

Augusta and Smith Henry worked hard all morning and into the afternoon, only to look outside to see visitors approaching. A large party was walking towards the house, which proved to be Edward, William and Lionel Bigg from The Hyde, as well as Mr Hallen and SIX DOGS! Just what they needed in the turmoil they were in. Augusta was quite upset that they should descend upon them in all their upheaval.

It took several weeks for the house to get straight and clean to Augusta's tolerable satisfaction. The continuing bad weather did not help. Abraham Dinnage was put to scrubbing Augusta's room and putting up her bed and wardrobe. The washhouse window was put in, and the kitchen and front door fitted. A new dresser and mantelpiece were put up, but the kitchen chimney was found to smoke too much.

The back room and the back kitchen were finished by Mr Hasson, and the other workmen cleared the cellars. Even when Mr and Mrs Cholmley called at the house on 9th October Augusta felt too ashamed at the state it was in to invite them inside; the upstairs rooms still being the only ones tolerably presentable. When the plasterers were called back on the 14th they made it as dirty as ever. Floor cloths arrived from Augusta's mother soon after, which made the hall more comfortable and some shelves were put up in the closet in the back hall. It was not until 21st October, when the drugget (a coarse woven fabric often used as a floor covering) was put down in the drawing room and the furniture re-arranged, that Augusta permitted herself to think they now had a room fit for visitors.

When November 5th arrived that year the family did not have a Guy Fawkes bonfire. Instead they were entertained at the front of the house by Henry and Abraham Dinnage who let off some squibs and crackers, much to the children's great delight. The day brought a difficult household problem for poor Augusta. Nurse was very distressed with her situation and broke down in floods of tears. No doubt the trauma of moving to such unprepared and miserable conditions, along with other things, had got on top of her. She poured out her soul to Augusta saying that she no longer felt satisfied with herself, that the children were getting above her and, as there was no prospect of another baby to attend to, she had better seek another situation. Augusta was sympathetic and spent time with Nurse trying to both reassure and console her. She cheered her up telling her how much she was needed, commenting that Caroline was of little or no use, while Rebecca was unsettled (understandably) because of the conditions in the kitchen. It still smoked dreadfully, it was draughty from all the doors, and was still lacking a larder, a dairy, a copper, a sink and a closet. But the remark passed that made Nurse much happier than anything else was Augusta's revelation to her that she was expecting another baby who, we shall learn later, turned out to be a fourth son, Frederick.

As the new house was being built throughout the year attention had been given to the estate, which was Smith Henry's domain. He bought two heifers, one with a calf and one expecting, in February, as well as some hens that soon produced a brood of nine chickens. Also in February the piece of ground allotted for the new garden was turned over for the first time. An entire field of black oats was sown at Easter, notwithstanding it poured all the time. Henry went to a sale of farm implements at this time hoping to purchase a land roller, but there was a wretched assortment and the roller went for 4/6p (22p), which he would not outbid. He had gone by coach to the sale, which was at Capel on the Dorking road about four miles north of Horsham. Although it was a wet evening, Smith Henry walked all the way home arriving very tired about 10.00pm. Disgruntled and disappointed he commented sourly to Augusta that there were four horses there with only two eyes between them. More crops were put in as the weather improved. By the end of March all their oats were in, about 15 acres in all, and the carrots and parsnips were being lined up to follow.

The children's interest in animals was encouraged by giving them chickens to call their own and to look after, and from The Hyde they brought three little rabbits for the children and three beagle puppies from their friend Captain Johnson. Pigs were added to the estate later on.

When the summer came it proved to be a traditional English summer, intermingling days of hot sunshine with wet days that caused frustration to the farm workers, as well as the children who liked nothing better than to join in the haymaking. The middle of July brought the Cattle Fair to Horsham and Smith Henry took young Henry, then 11 years old, along to look the stock over and to enjoy the experience. Unfortunately, the lambs that were needed at Swallowfield were too expensive, there being too many buyers in the market that day, so they came back empty-handed.

Smith Henry and Augusta were hopeful of a good harvest, but again they were disappointed when July turned wet, and remained so. The poor weather continued into the first half of August, by which time the wheat and the other crops were in a bad way. It wasn't until the third week in August that a start was made to cutting the oats, but it was more a case of working whenever the weather permitted than planning in an orderly fashion. The disaster which had looked likely, however, did not transpire and in the end a reasonably satisfactory crop of oats, wheat and barley was cut and stored by the first week of September. The crop that was particularly good that year was the apple, with varieties such as Ribstones, Golden Knob and Quarander being plentiful in the orchard. The apple crop was so abundant that 30 bushels of cider were made in November.

During the autumn, laurels, holly and berberis were purchased and planted in front of the house, and further shrubs were brought over from The Hyde.

As autumn of 1845 turned to winter the seasonal work continued. More wheat was drilled, and oats were threshed. In the farmyard, Henry was busy pulling down the shed to set it further back, and additional shrubs were planted. Augusta had been complaining to Smith Henry about the state of the pathways across the common to the north of Swallowfield, at Mannings Heath, and although she believed nothing would be done, she had obviously left her mark. While out shooting one day in December, he made up his mind that a road would have to be built and two days later he had set men to work to do just that. Poor Smith Henry, having dutifully responded to Augusta's demands he now found himself in trouble with the authorities, in the person of a Mr Padwick, who wrote to him immediately to point out the error of his actions. The building of a road was a trespass on the common, and he was begged to desist from further work and to reinstate the work already commissioned. A call on Mr Padwick proved fruitless, as he was not at home.

Augusta regarded her faith as being very important to her and was determined that the children should be brought up with a similar, strong conviction. Throughout her life she attended church regularly and was attentive to the events and services that she participated in. She worshipped at St. Mary's, Horsham's parish church, walking there from her temporary home and back in all weathers, usually with one or more of the children. The Revd. Hodgson was the vicar at St. Mary's. He had been there for just over four years in 1845: he was to stay for another 39 years! Augusta's diaries mention how he was always keen to join in cricket matches, and to play football with the youngsters of the parish. St.Mary's was built as a consequence of expansion in Horsham in the 19th century, coinciding with religious revival. (Horsham's population at this time was in the order of 5,000.) The Revd. Hodgson was assisted by the Revd. Jarvis Kenrick from 1842, in the capacity of Curate. Both are regularly mentioned by Augusta. She also attended the 'new' church, as she called it, which was St. Mark's, North Street, also in the centre of Horsham. At the time she knew it, St. Mark's did not have a spire as that was a later addition. (As Horsham's present residents will observe with some irony, all we have now on the site of the old St. Mark's is the spire and no church!) Once the family had moved into Swallowfield they started going to church at St. Andrew's, Nuthurst, which was only a mile or so down the road leading from Monks Gate, or Monk's Common as it was then known. Walking along this road to St. Andrew's one day Augusta noticed new hedges being put in which were intended to produce a great quantity of faggots, hoops and broomsticks for which she thought there seemed to be high demand at the time.

Augusta and her family had to walk virtually everywhere up until May, as they had no carriage of their own and the omnibus service was not very convenient for them. It was brother Edward who loaned them a chaise which, with a little contrivance, they managed to put in the coach house at Swallowfield. That improved things no end for Smith Henry and Augusta.[3]

Visits between the families at Swallowfield and the Hyde were frequent, usually twice or three times a week. Either Smith Henry would ride over to go hunting with the beagles, or fishing in the lakes, or shooting in the woods and fields. In return, Edward and the other brothers and sisters who lived at The Hyde would come over in one of their carriages to pay their respects. The Penny Post had been introduced nationally five years earlier, so it was easy to drop an invitation in the post, rather than to have one of the servants carry it over by hand.

The children were enthusiastic about their new home, but suffered a little because of its shortcomings in comfort and warmth. It was all right in the fine weather, when doors and windows were open to let in the fresh air, but it was quite a different story in the cold and wind of winter.

3. Forms of transport varied considerably in these times. The gentry had four-horse carriages; private carriages, traps and chaises were used for shopping. Traders would use four horses, or six horses to pull their wagons. Augusta writes in her diary of seeing a ten-horse team in Horsham at one point. Dog carts were sometimes used, the animals being harnessed three abreast.

Attendance at school for all children was not compulsory in those times and did not become so until the Education Act was passed in 1870. There were two types of public school in existence in 1845. In 1811 the Church of England had formed; *"...the National Society for Promoting the Education of the Poor in the Principles of the Established Church"* the so called National schools.

The second type was started up three years later by the Non-Conformist bodies, who had already founded the British and Commonwealth Schools Society. Their 'British schools' were set up following the formation of; *"...the Institute for promoting the Education of the Labouring and Manufacturing Classes of Society of Every Religious Persuasion."*

There was a National school at Nuthurst at this time, it having been opened in 1824, but this was not for Henry.[4]

In 1845 the eldest of the children, Henry, reached the age of 11. He was packed off to boarding school in Brighton in January, and only came back for the holidays. Smith Henry missed him a great deal and tried to spend as much time with Henry as he could whenever he was back at Swallowfield. Father and son would happily go off fishing, or hunting with their dogs, whenever the opportunity arose. Young Henry wrote to his Mother and Father regularly from Brighton, and we hear of his health from Miss Millar his schoolmistress. She told Augusta in January by letter that Henry was suffering a good deal from skin irritation and spots, but Augusta was more dismayed to learn of his disinclination to learn Latin! Augusta was very much aware of Henry's weak chest and stayed in touch with the school to make enquiries about his health. On a more practical note, she made sure young Henry had a cake for his birthday in May, as well as his paint box, both of which were sent down by Fullers carrier service some weeks in advance. This seems to have encouraged the youngster, as a note by return asked for a new hat, or cap, and some gum - presumably of the adhesive type rather than for chewing. His letter home of 17th April made mention of progress with his Latin, which was endorsed by a very satisfactory letter from Miss Millar, who said that Henry was quite well and much grown. More to the point, he had been much more attentive to his schooling, and his improvement should be evident. Unfortunately, by the time December came that year the family's fortunes were at such a low ebb as far as money was concerned that Augusta closes her diary for the year with the following comment about Henry and his education.

"We have been obliged among other grievances to keep Henry away from school, which is a sad thing for him as he is so very backward. But I endeavour to get him more perfect in his Latin grammar and English lessons; Edward is very nearly as forward as he is. Augusta is as steady as ever and learns all her lessons and is anxious to get on. Little William does nothing but play."

This is, apparently, another reflection of the state of the family's finances.

Daughter Augusta, who had her 10th birthday in May 1845, and was the second eldest child, had not gone away to school. She stayed at Swallowfield and enjoyed the exciting

4. *By 1846-7 there were both girls' and boys' National schools, each with a paid teacher, and with 79 pupils in all.*

St. Andrew's, Nuthurst in 1805, from a watercolour by Geoffrey Sharpe. The restoration of the church did not take place until 1856, so Smith Henry and Augusta would have known it at first without its spire.
Sussex Archaeological Society, Lewes

St. Andrew's sketched by W. Quartermain in 1859, following its restoration. *Photocopy, Norman Hempstead.*

experiences of living on a big country estate along with her two younger brothers, Edward two years younger than her and young William, approaching his fourth birthday.

And so we come to the end of 1845 for Smith Henry and Augusta, pregnant with her fifth and last child, and their young family. A year which saw them venture to a new home in Sussex, but beset by financial worries, no doubt occasioned by their trying to emulate brother Edward and his estate at The Hyde. Augusta's final entry in her diary for the year comments;

"We are now arrived at the end of the year in which we have received many blessings. We are all well in health but I trust if we are spared to see the end of another year it will find us more comfortable in our house and finances, our building and our farm together having led us into a great many expenses which we cannot get over for some time to come but we must bear it as well as we can and hope for the best."

This reflective comment of Augusta's is one we will see mirrored by others as our story of Swallowfield unfolds.

We will now follow in turn the fortunes of each of the five children of Smith Henry and Augusta. First, in Chapter 3 the eldest son Henry, the one least inclined to learning, and the one with the poor chest, and see where his fortunes take him. Then, in Chapter 4, we will follow the only daughter Augusta, with the same name as her mother. Chapters 5, 6 and 7 take us on in time with the other three boys - Edward, William and Frederick.

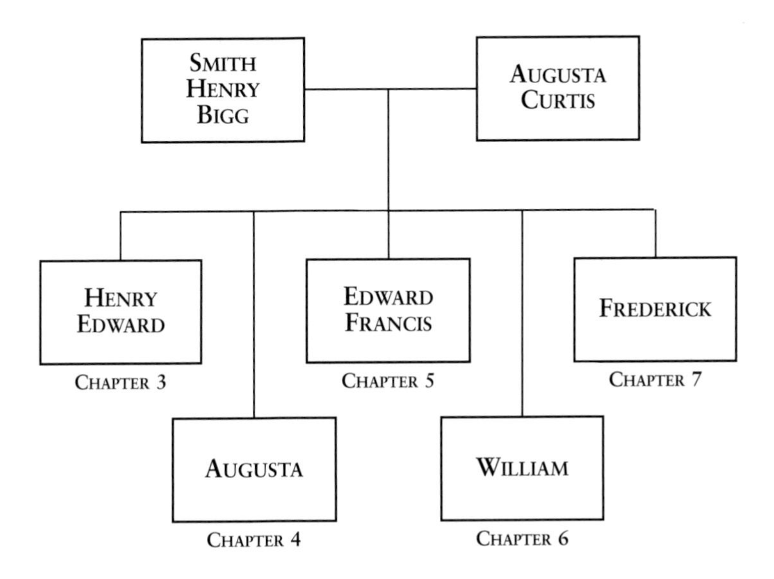
Smith
Henry
Bigg
Augusta
Curtis
Henry
Edward
Chapter 3
Edward
Francis
Chapter 5
Frederick
Chapter 7
Augusta
Chapter 4
William
Chapter 6

Chart 3

CHAPTER THREE
HENRY'S STORY

The Bigg family, Smith Henry, Augusta and the children settled into their new home at Swallowfield, where Frederick was born on 8th July, 1846; the family were to be together there for the next ten years.

Henry continued to be plagued by bronchitis throughout his school days, and this had an effect upon his education because of the interruptions it caused. At Swallowfield he obtained a good grounding in farm work, learned to shoot with some success and took part in the usual social activities of riding and hunting. These were to stand him in good stead in years to come. By the time he was 21 his mother was complaining that

"Henry didn't seem to settle to any permanent work and would sooner go with his friends to Brighton to watch the cricket".

Then Henry, at the age of 22, left the family home and sailed for Australia.

Emigrating in 1856, after a bad winter, the eldest son left his family and went to seek a new life for himself on the other side of the world. His departure was due to his mother's insistence. She had been warned by doctors that Henry's health was such that he would not be able to stand more English winters, because of his bronchitis and bad colds. He would have to go to warmer climes. And so, when Mrs Marsh - a friend - told Augusta that her son owned property in New England, New South Wales and was always looking for reliable young men to work at Salisbury Court, 11km south of Uralla, the die was cast, and Henry was despatched without delay. Although the family knew that it was sensible to send Henry away to the better climate Australia could offer, it must have been a heartbreaking wrench for his parents and for his four younger brothers and sister. Before leaving he gave his pigeons to his young brother William to look after, and on 18th December 1856 William and his father

"took the half past 8 o'clock train to take a last look at Little Henry".

While the climate in Australia was undoubtedly much more suitable to Henry's health, the environment no doubt came as a surprise to the young man. After a journey by ship of several weeks with time for relaxation and contemplation aplenty, he arrived in Sydney NSW and suddenly found himself thrust into a burgeoning new colony, where hard work and physical effort were the order of the day. Not quite Henry's scene, you might think; he is described as being more of a dreamer than a practical man.

Australia was still a relatively young colony. The practice of transporting convicts to NSW had ceased in 1840, but by the time Henry arrived seventeen years later the population of New South Wales was increasing dramatically, following the discovery of gold near Bathurst in 1851. The population of Australia in 1851 was only 437,665, but by 1858 it would grow to 1 million. The impact of gold fever in the early 1850s had a considerable effect on the economy, as might be expected. It was the wool growers who ultimately gained from the rapid increase in population and local purchasing-power. The demand for meat increased the value of sheep and created a new market for cattle. New roads had to be built to carry traffic to the mining areas, ships with larger capacity were necessary to cope with increased import demands, which meant that the shipowners were anxious to get return cargoes. Wool was what they carried away from Australia, and a rise in the world price of wool meant that the trade was good. A downside of gold fever was the way folk simply 'upped sticks' and left for the goldfields; at the beginning of 1852 there were only two policemen in Melbourne, the rest had gone to look for gold!

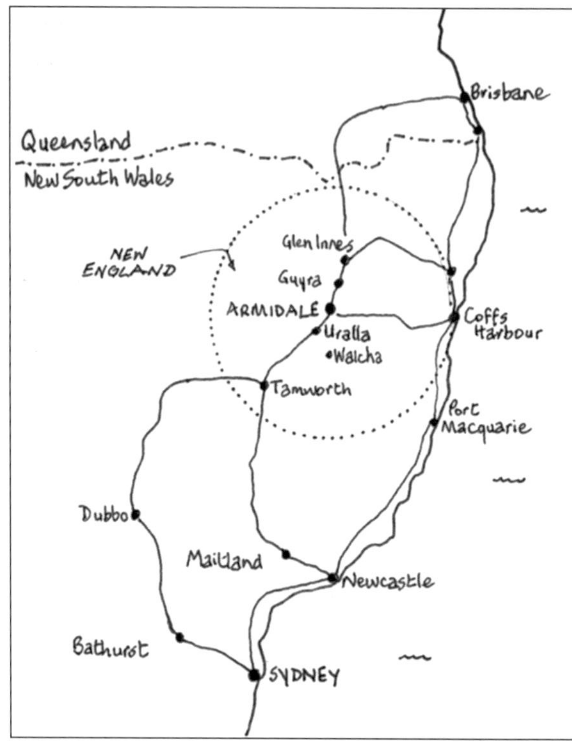

New England area 350 miles north of Sydney

Landing at Sydney Henry stayed first at Camden with Henry and Sarah Burnell, who had emigrated to Australia in 1828. His maternal grandmother was a Burnell, and the Burnells were kin of the Curtis family who are to feature so prominently in our story a little later on. He also stayed at their dairy farm at Kings Cross. He then made his way to Mr Marsh's property Salisbury Court, Uralla, where on the 13th April 1857 a note was entered in the farm diary *'Bigg arrived today'*.

By all accounts Henry had a tough four years ahead of him. It isn't clear whether he started as a jackeroo, or just a learner. At that time only 40 acre blocks were allowable as freehold, so most landholders had sheep and cattle spread over wide areas on leasehold. Mobs were always on the track. Moving stock from the Hunter to near Brisbane, Henry was a part of the droving outfit. He got his keep, but had to provide his own saddle and horses.

One trip he is supposed to have made was with another employee to Port Macquarie to collect 40 rams that came from Sydney by ship. It must have been quite a task getting them up the narrow track through dense forest over the escarpment to Salisbury Court.

While mustering sheep at Salisbury Court in 1859 he had a fall from his horse, resulting in concussion and a broken leg. The Burraston family living and working the place took

5. The Revd. Septimus Hungerford had an enormous parish and was constantly travelling on horseback to all parts of it.

him in and nursed him back to health. Within a year he had married. His wife was Anne (Annie) Burraston, oldest daughter of the James and Catherine Burraston who had looked after him after the accident. James' profession is given as Wool Sorter. Annie was said to be a strong, practical woman who kept his feet on the ground. Marrying Annie was the best thing Henry ever did, according to his contemporaries, and that's easy to acknowledge.

The couple were married on 6th February 1860 at the Burraston's house by the Revd. Septimus Hungerford of Armidale, the Church of England parish clergyman.[5] As the Burrastons were strong Catholics this must have involved some interesting 'negotiations'!

Apparently, very soon after their wedding the couple went off droving sheep to Rockhampton, in Queensland, as Henry's expenses for this drive are recorded in the estate accounts. Rockhampton is well over 1000 km from Armidale as the crow flies, so it was quite an unusual honeymoon, to say the least.

Conditions in the tropics are now recognised as being very hard and not really suitable for sheep, although Henry is on record as shearing 1,000 sheep at Gracemere, about 10km south-west of Rockhampton, from where wool was shipped to England.

Our 'Little Henry' seems to have grown to be a fine, strong man by now. How his parents would have loved to have seen him, but none of the family from England ever came out to Australia to visit Henry and his wife and to see for themselves the arduous conditions they had to work in. But Augusta, his mother, was very supportive, sending him £10 as often as she could, which was a great help. Knowing what we do about the parlous state of Smith Henry and Augusta's finances in the early days, we can only assume that things had got a little better over the ensuing years. £10 was a fine sum in the 1860s, equivalent to £750-800 in 1999 terms.

Henry and Annie had three children. First to be born to Henry and Annie was a son, Frederick, four days after Christmas Day 1860 at Rockhampton. Unfortunately, young Frederick was struck down with diphtheria just over three years later and died at their home near Isaac's River, north of Rockhampton in March 1864.

On 6th December 1862 a second son had been born, and named Alfred Edward. He was born somewhere between Rockhampton and Mount Morgan and the birth was not formally registered as such until a travelling parson 'rounded up' a number of children <u>two years later</u> and made up a baptism certificate. (The phrase 'rounded up' seems to catch the mood of the times quite well.) This lack of a registered birth certificate was to cause many problems for Alfred in later years when he came to inherit at various times; to the bureaucrats he was a non-person.

Henry and Annie were blessed with a daughter, Augusta Emily, on 22nd June 1864. (This is the third Augusta we have come across, and there are more.) She became known as 'Amy', so this is what we will call her in this narrative.

By June of 1865 Henry, Annie and their two surviving children had left Queensland and moved back to Uralla, where they bought a 40 acre block of land, about 3km to the south of the township, near the racecourse lagoon. A further two blocks of land, each of similar size, were soon bought in the same locality.

Over the course of the next 9 years, between 1866 and 1875, Henry and Annie kept in touch with Smith Henry and Augusta (his mother and father) back home in Swallowfield in Sussex by a regular exchange of correspondence. These letters from Henry and Annie give an insight into the desperate struggle they had to raise a family and work the land productively. Augusta wrote constantly in her diaries about the news she was receiving from Uralla.[6]

Here are some extracts:

LETTER FROM HENRY DATED 10TH DECEMBER 1866.

This is a good season, rain seems to come when it is wanted and my trees and crops are growing splendidly. Wheat is the worst, though it is high and looks well it seems half smut. I shall now have plenty of wheat for our own consumption. I am in great spirits with the Paddock: the number of horses keeps increasing, sometimes 10, sometimes 20 and I expect to get more. The valuable cows are a failure so far, two died but pigs pay well. I can sell them or the bacon as fast as I can breed them. In fact I should make money this year only the expense of building and fencing was so great that it is not all paid off yet. Amongst the seeds you sent me the peas did best. Our little girl's name is Augusta Emily but I think she will always be called Amy as that is what she calls herself.

LETTER FROM ANNIE DATED 6TH FEBRUARY 1867.

We are none of us well, the weather has been so hot and dry, the crops are all burnt up and the garden sadly in need of rain. The wheat was got up in good order but we only had a small quantity and Henry does not consider it a paying crop. We had a little dance here on New Year's Eve, quite a small affair. We seldom see the clergyman as he lives 20 miles off and only preaches every fortnight at Uralla. He is the same person who married us 7 years ago today. In May next year I shall be 26 though most people think I do not look that. Henry is turning grey, he is too anxious and it is making him an old man. If we make a living it is quite as much as we shall - fortunes are not to be made by farming, still we have no room for complaint, for we have been more fortunate than most people. I have a nice lot of young fowls and we are able to make our own butter.

Our garden has been a great benefit to us. I am very well off for reading, it is very easy to get nice books and I read a great deal. The little ones are out of my way now and are very little trouble in fine weather when they can get out to play. The Misses Marsh drove over one day - such nice girls - one had been to Sydney to see Mrs Burnell and her family.

LETTER FROM ANNIE AUGUST 1867.
Henry has had very fair crops and some melons weighing 26lbs each.

DIARY ENTRY FOR 22ND SEPTEMBER 1867 - FOLLOWING A LETTER FROM AUSTRALIA.

Annie says they are getting poorer every day, they are £100 in debt and have no prospect of paying it. Clothing is so dear and farm produce will hardly sell at the lowest prices. Annie's brother James does not live with them but he and his brother Joseph

6. *Remember that her diary dates are several weeks, sometimes months, after the letters were posted from Australia, because all mail had to come by sea. The average voyage time alone was 3 months in those times, before allowing for collection at one end and delivery at the other. It was shorter after the Suez canal was opened in 1869, although not all vessels sailing to and from Australia would be using it.*

lend Henry a hand now and then and he keeps their horses for them as he cannot afford to pay them any other way.

DIARY ENTRY FOR 30TH OCTOBER 1867.

Henry writes in better spirits and says they are all in a state of nervous excitement there being a report of a new goldfield having been found close to them. If true, he says,

"it will be the making of us all. I shall grow tons of melons for the diggers and shall doubtless have my paddock full of horses at an increased price per head. I now have 100 fruit trees, all choice sorts and a perfect forest of English and American trees".

DIARY ENTRY IN DECEMBER 1867.

Henry enters upon his money affairs - also about Clandon about which he knows nothing. I think it would be of no use to write to him about it as he can do nothing and could not raise even a £5 note. He hopes his father will not spend anything on it unless it will be of some benefit to him. He hoped he should have been able to pay off the money he owed, contracted in fencing and building but the great fall in farm produce made that hope a delusion.

"I make a very good living here enough to pay all present expenses but I cannot pay up arrears (altogether £160) and I am much afraid I shall be sold off as they call it. I was thinking if it would be very wrong to ask Aunt Tite (his mother's sister Emily married a wealthy architect Sir William Tite) to lend it to me as I should be able to pay it back some day and I have no doubt she would lend it to me, the only thing is whether it would be right to ask her after all her kindness to me. I had made up my mind to write to her this mail but I thought I would ask your advice first they say it is better to be born lucky than rich but it is certainly inconvenient to be born neither."

"He then tells me he is going on a jury for which he gets a few shillings though not many but he likes going as it is a change and he hears a little law."What should we have done without Edward Bigg's £100 and the valuable content of the box".[7]I hope he will be more happy and it will give him the spirits to persevere.

AUGUSTA'S LETTER TO AUNT LUCY (SMITH HENRY'S OLDER SISTER) JANUARY 1868.

Henry says he intends to try sheep again as soon as he possibly can even if it is only a few. Now he has a few nice cattle and if he sees a good opportunity he shall sell some of them and buy some sheep.

DIARY ENTRY IN MARCH 1868.

Henry says Uncle John (Mother's brother John Curtis-Ed.) had just sent him a letter of credit for £10 which was very kind and quite unasked for - indeed it rather annoys him that he should know he was in want of it, as he does not often tell his wants to anyone.

7. *Edward was Henry's father's brother, living at The Hyde. The Box was a huge Christmas box sent every year to Henry and his family. In fact we would probably regard it as a crate knowing the contents of it in some years. To Henry and Annie it must have been more than just a normal Christmas present, as it inevitably included things they desperately needed, like clothes, shoes, materials and furniture.* *(See diary entry for 25th January 1870, overleaf.)*

"In fact I cannot consider myself badly off as we live very comfortably here and this place pays very fairly. I had four acres of good wheat, quite 40 bushels to the acre and I am sure it will weigh 64lbs to the bushel. I have plenty of grass and a good many horses on it". Then he speaks of the races which are held close to them and kept them alive for two days as the grandstand and all the booths for selling grog etc are close to his garden. The course is round the lake, a mile and a half. Annie writes some days later and speaks of a terrific storm, the trees being torn up by their roots and greatly damaging the crops. Then summer was going and they all seem to dread the winter.

DIARY ENTRY IN MAY 1868 - FOLLOWING A LETTER FROM ANNIE TO HENRY'S SISTER.

She says they are all in very good health and spirits. Alfred is such a dear little fellow and so superior to any child she sees. Amy is not the least like him, so wild and full of spirits. They are very thankful to Uncle Bigg for the money and she owns - though Henry did not - that it was sadly needed.

DIARY ENTRY IN JULY 1868.

The ship carrying 'the Box' has been sighted off Melbourne.

DIARY ENTRY ON 7TH AUGUST 1868.

Henry was afraid Annie had some complaint coming in her eye but as three years ago she had a similar spot in the other eye and it disappeared he hopes it may be the case with this one. They have heard of the safety of the Box. Four weeks ago they saw in the paper that the ship had arrived after an unheard-of long passage and it was stated in the list of goods that there was one for J. McCrossin, so I hope they had it soon.[8]

DIARY ENTRY IN SEPTEMBER 1868.

The Box has arrived and has been seven months getting there, they think the children were more pleased with the clock than anything. "They had seen one before but never heard one strike and they think it a great wonder and several times a day they come running to us to say the clock has struck". Henry thinks the clock and the slippers the greatest luxuries and they both seem much pleased with the patchwork counterpane. Of course Annie's letter was all on the same subject - how delighted they were with the content of the Box, the things were all so good and everything of use. "The little suits of clothes for Alfred are such a nice fit and he is proud of them. The chairs which Augusta sent are in constant use and Amy's little frocks fit nicely and I am not likely to have to make any up for a long time". I am very sorry she complains of her eyes and she says she misses Augusta's nice letters. I must write a few lines to her in my letter to Henry just going.

(There is no diary for the period Oct 1868-July 1869)

8. *McCrossin was also the handling agent dealing with the Bill of Lading, the family living for many years in Uralla. Incidentally, McCrossin's mill and forge was bought by Henry's grandson 25 years ago and put back on its feet and is in production still.*

DIARY ENTRY IN AUGUST 1869.

Annie says Henry is very well but very thin and looking old for his years. Alfred gets on very well at school - he has two miles to walk morning and evening which does not seem to tire him in the least. Amy was 5 years old on the 22nd June, a fine child so merry and engaging.

DIARY ENTRY IN OCTOBER 1869.

Henry says that his farm is now 20 acres larger than ours and is farmed most artistically with the help of one man and not always that. He has only 5 acres under crops, wheat, barley, potatoes, Indian corn and pumpkins – I always thought he had but 40 acres. He seems to write cheerfully.

DIARY ENTRY IN OCTOBER 1869.

Henry says that a great many diamonds have been found out there lately and most of the gold-digging population were seeking for them. One man lately found one of great size, larger than the Koohinoor [9], which he took to Sydney and exhibited at 2/6d per head until excitement was sufficiently raised to form a company to buy it. They gave him £400 by way of a beginning. It was found to be no diamond and the finder disappeared.

DIARY ENTRY IN DECEMBER 1869.

The Australian letters were satisfactory. They are very pleased at the thought of another Box being sent out. Henry only mentions trousering, a steel rat-trap and some tennis balls. Annie wants an album and riding skirt and the little boy knows that I will send him some nice things. Henry seems pretty well and free from cough, always busy in the garden which he keeps very nice.

DIARY ENTRY IN JANUARY 1870.

Poor Annie's letter was of different import: she says they are going downhill for as they are making nothing they must get more involved every day and they fear they will be obliged to part with their house. I wish we could help them. (At this time Smith Henry and Augusta were in no position to help them, as we shall see.)

DIARY ENTRY ON 25TH JANUARY 1870.

Lucy was very distressed at Annie's letter and sent Henry £60. She says *"I do sincerely hope that it may arrive in time to prevent his selling the little place he now has, for it would be a dreadful thing for himself and family to be wandering about again without a roof to cover them". (A reference to their wanderings in Queensland.) She later called after lunch with valuable contributions to the Box in addition to the money which I never expected: 42 yds calico, 20 yds flannel, a dress, a cloak, a Whittle, 2 shirts, boots etc.*

DIARY ENTRY IN MARCH 1870.

Henry is shortly going droving again as he has to make money somehow. He has been particularly unfortunate this year, he lost four draught horses and a hailstorm destroyed

9. The Koh-i-noor to give it its proper name, had been presented to the British Crown regalia by the East India Company in 1850.

his wheat. Little boy gets on at school and had a prize. Henry tells us about the new Ministry which he fears will be no better than the last.

DIARY ENTRY IN APRIL 1870.

Poor Annie says she has been ill for some time and was only gaining strength slowly when she wrote (17th Jan). Henry had just started on his journey to Maitland taking stock for Mr Marsh and another. A letter written a month later speaks of her bad health and a fearful hot summer. The children are a great comfort to her. Poor little boy was so disappointed at not having a letter from me and sends another written in ink. She encloses a letter from Henry written a fortnight after he left in which he was getting on well barring bad eyes. He seems in pretty good spirits and seems to have some project in his head after the job he has is over. Poor Boy, he has worked very hard. How pleased he will be to get Uncle Bigg's and Aunt Lucy's present. I wish he could get something to do which would bring him in a little money and I hope Annie will give better account of herself.

DIARY ENTRY IN JULY 1870.

A letter from Henry to Aunt Lucy, thanking her for the present which he says gladdened his eyes. He wishes for his own credit he could tell her he was doing better but it is not the case at present but he still lives in hope.

DIARY ENTRY IN SEPTEMBER 1870.

They had heard of the safety of the Box which was sent on 5th Feb. All well.

DIARY ENTRY IN NOVEMBER 1870.

Henry in good spirits, he is going to continue in the sheep business. He is not selling any now on account of the wet weather which made them fall off and he found travelling and camping out at night too severe for him but the spring was coming on and he would begin again. He wants me to tell him in my next letter the average weight of the Southdowns as he wants to get a few English sheep.

DIARY ENTRY IN FEBRUARY 1871.

Henry speaks of the continued rain which has now lasted 9 months and the whole country is a vast swamp, swollen rivers and waterfalls but he still thinks it is better than the fearful droughts they have had. The war created great excitement out there and causes a disturbing effect on the wool market, even in his small way (150 sheep). It will make a difference of £7-£8. He has taken Alfred away from school for a time as he does not think he is getting on and the weather is so very bad, he is always getting wet and he finds him very useful at home. He rides on horseback and can trot and canter as well as Henry can.

(Alfred would have been 8 years old at this time.)

JUNE 1871.

Henry says he had a very severe attack on the lungs a short time ago, he could only breathe with intense pain but he was all right when he wrote (18th April). He cured himself with mustard plasters on each side of his ribs, inhaled steam from a jug of hot water and took any quantity of senna. He is thankful to say that it is seldom any of them are ill and considering what an invalid he once was says he is wonderfully strong now. He doesn't say what he is doing.

On the 17th February 1871 Smith Henry's older brother, Barrister Edward Smith Bigg who lived at The Hyde in Sussex, a few miles away from Swallowfield, passed away at the age of 71. He was a bachelor and therefore what would happen to The Hyde and his wealth on his death was a matter of great interest to family members. It would only become known when the Will was read. As it transpired, The Hyde passed down to a nephew, Henry's younger brother Edward Francis. The estate was to be distributed to all his nephews and nieces after Lucy died. Lucy was then aged 72, unmarried and living at The Hyde. She and Smith Henry were the only surviving children of Edward and Sarah Bigg. It is surprising that Edward Smith Bigg did not pass on The Hyde to his brother Smith Henry, or Smith Henry's eldest son Henry in Australia, but left it instead to Edward, Smith Henry's second son. Why he did this we can only surmise. He would have known Smith Henry was by now reasonably well settled at Swallowfield, and maybe he worried somewhat about Smith Henry's track record with financial affairs. Perhaps he felt doubtful about Smith Henry's ability to manage the valuable estate competently. And then there was Henry in Australia, his nephew. Would he be the right person to take on responsibility for the magnificent Hyde estate. Hardly, he was struggling from one enterprise to another, earning a few pounds here and there, now and again, and then spending what he made somewhat incautiously on new ideas that came to nothing. No, was the answer to that option probably. So who else?

The next nephew, Edward, was a different character, more stable and conventional in many respects. Edward had stayed behind to support his father at Swallowfield, but had still found time to get properly educated and qualified. And he had chosen to pursue the same profession as his Uncle, the Law. At 33 years of age, a steady and reliable sort, recently married, with good prospects, and someone he knew thoroughly because they lived in close proximity, his namesake young Edward must have seemed the appropriate choice.

DIARY ENTRY IN AUGUST 1871.

Henry has just heard of Uncle's death, he thinks we are unfairly dealt with but as regards his not getting The Hyde he is not the least disappointed or surprised - he always felt sure Edward would have it and it gives him great happiness to think of the good fortune that has befallen him.

LETTER FROM ANNIE TO AUGUSTA, SEPTEMBER 1871 - AS RECORDED IN HER DIARY.

"Henry works hard but there is little progress, in fact we are far behind and there is nothing to be made on a farm unless you have plenty to start with and can afford to keep stock, that is the only thing that pays". Alfred is going to school again and she thinks he will be a clever boy. She still complains of her eyes.

From Henry:

"We are very much involved nor do I see any way of getting out of it"

without parting with their place. Annie had been very poorly and Amy has had a bad attack of dysentery. The little boy writes he is much improved in his writing.

DIARY ENTRY IN OCTOBER 1871.

Henry says to a certain extent the sheep business was a failure as it did not realise the extensive profit that he had anticipated, nothing he takes in hand does so, so he is used to it but altogether they paid pretty well and now he is breeding from 100 of them and he has 200 more getting fat.

DIARY ENTRY IN DECEMBER 1871.

Annie has been laid up for 10 days in bed, better now but frightfully thin and weak. The children are well and strong. Alfred works hard in the garden and when not at school devotes his entire evening to reading 'Line upon Line' and Amy is getting on.

DIARY ENTRY IN MARCH 1872 - ABOUT A LETTER OF 1ST NOVEMBER THE PREVIOUS YEAR.

Henry writes, just after Mr Marsh's funeral.[10] *It was the largest ever seen in Armidale, 21 carriages and buggies and 100 on horseback. Henry says no one was more sorry to lose him than he was, he esteemed him very much but he was always unfortunate in money affairs. His friends are subscribing a memorial window in the Church. Henry gave 10/- and wished he could afford to give more. His brother allowed him £1,000 a year to manage the large property out there but he always lived up to his means if not beyond it and his family are left with nothing. Henry says he has been doing better the last year than he has ever done but he has owed £100 for some time and after considering a whole month he wrote to Aunt Tite to ask her to lend him that sum because he knows if he lives he will be able to pay it back again and we know his aunt did kindly send him out that sum. His cough keeps gradually reducing him in weight, he used to weigh 9 stone and that is little enough but now he is only 8 stone. Alfred is growing very tall and strong. Henry doesn't consider him forward for his age (9 years) but he is very persevering.*

DIARY ENTRY IN APRIL 1872.

Henry is setting out on another expedition taking 2,000 sheep to Maitland and bringing back about 20 imported ones for a station near them. He has made up his mind not to do any more of this work as it is very laborious and trying but necessity obliges and he has always made more by that than by anything else. He expects to be away about 9 weeks and hopes to clear £20. His father in law is going to stay at his place and look after everything while he is away, he has 300 sheep of his own. Annie writes the other half of the letter ten days after and is in very bad spirits. She never likes his going away and his health has been so bad for some time that she dreads the effects of camping out. The little girl, too, has been under the care of the doctor for some time with pains in her head and chest and she is so anxious about her, she is so delicate (which I never heard before). She says her eyes are very bad at night so that she can hardly see to write and it grieves me to hear such a poor account of them.

10. *Mr Marsh, of Salisbury Court, Uralla, had employed the young Henry Bigg soon after his arrival in NSW, back in 1857.*

DIARY ENTRY IN MAY 1872.

Augusta forwarded a letter from Uralla, Henry had returned from his journey to Maitland and says he was glad enough to be back again and has undergone great hardships from the heat and scarcity of water. There was little feed for the sheep and none for the horses, one died out of three. Also two dogs but he did pretty well making £1 a day for 50 days and then bought 300 sheep and he was going to travel with them for sale and he hopes it will answer. He will not be away from home for so long. Annie says that Amy has been very ill but was now better though very pale and thin. Alfred quite well and growing so fast he is much taller than any boy of his age about there and she thinks he will be very good looking.

DIARY ENTRY IN JUNE 1872.

Henry was away nine weeks and made £24 but it was dearly earned money and he hopes he shall not have occasion to go any more. He does not think he is the worse for it; he was just going off again on a different undertaking. Tin is being found in large quantities in New England lately and much near where he lives, so he with his wife's brother James were going to start with pack horses and a complete digger's outfit and a great roll of blankets. Mineral land is bought from the Government at 5/- the acre and his idea if he should be fortunate enough to find tin, merely to buy the land and sell it again.

DIARY ENTRY IN SEPTEMBER 1872.

The ship "The Maid of Judith" had arrived in Sydney so they hope they may get the Box soon and the children are getting very excited about it.[11] *There have been enormous finds of tin in New England and it is expected there will be a great population there before long. Mr Marsh's station is nearly all tin, much is let out in patches on a seven years lease and the house is sold for an hotel. Henry says if he had nothing better to do he should go out for a good exploration and persevere until he found a mine of tin or gold or some metal but he cannot do that without giving up his present business. His sheep are doing well.*

DIARY ENTRY IN OCTOBER 1872.

The Box has arrived in good order and they were delighted with everything. Alfred wore his new suit of clothes at Church and looked so well in them.

DIARY ENTRY IN JANUARY 1873.

They have received the £10 Augusta (her daughter and Henry's sister) sent out and it was most acceptable. Henry says, "How I do wish I was out of pecuniary want, I would much sooner earn money myself than have it given to me but my schemes and speculations (though of late rather more successful than usual) never come up to my expectations." He is now going to try the "carrying business" and is in treaty for two drays and teams. Annie says that Henry looks so well and is in good spirits and she

11. *The vessel was not "The Maid of Judith" but the "Maid Judah". She was a ship of 756 tons built in Aberdeen in 1853, and sold by the Aberdeen Line to Cowlishaw Bros., Sydney in 1870. Her Master was Captain D. Bain and she sailed from Aberdeen on March 21st 1872, arriving in Sydney on June 23rd that year. The "Maid" was broken up in 1880.*

thinks their affairs are more prosperous than they have been for some time. They have a nice lot of lambs, they had just sold their sheepskins well and were going out to shear again. They are building very much near them and in all sorts of out of the way places where 12 months ago there wasn't a white man to be seen.

DIARY ENTRY IN MARCH 1873.

Henry says he is full of troubles as usual and consequently rather out of spirits. Amy had run a needle into her foot and she must have suffered frightfully as it was in her foot for two days before it was taken out. They were obliged to take her to Armidale, a good two days' journey, have her foot lanced to the bone and have the needle taken out with a pair of tweezers. She was obliged to be chloroformed. It was a month ago and the child has no use of her foot yet. Another trouble is that the sheep are all dying from the constant rains and Henry gets so out of spirits with their repeated failures. They have had sad uphill work for many years.

DIARY ENTRY IN MAY 1873.

A letter from Alfred who is much improved in his writing and says he got the second prize in second class and he does not ride the pony now because she tumbles down with him but he rides the big horse that is very quiet and he can make bows and arrows and fire them too. Henry says his sheep are not doing any better and all over New England they are dying off. On Mr Marsh's station they are losing 300 a week. The last three years have been very wet and the last year it has rained nearly every day, and the week before he said Sydney was nearly washed away, 15 inches of rain fell in 24 hours.[12] *Annie says Amy's foot is quite well and she is now sent to school.*

DIARY ENTRY IN MAY 1873 - *talking about a letter from a Captain Donkin to his mother, that was forwarded to Augusta. Tom Donkin gives a very graphic account of his journeys from Newcastle to Bendemeer, about 30 hours by rail and omnibus, having left his wife in Sydney. He says:*

"We were drawing near to that part of the road where Henry said he would meet us when a gentleman and two children hove in sight. The coachman pulled up and the gentleman spoke: "Have you a passenger by the name of Captain Donkin?" Then I knew him to be Henry Bigg. He looked very old and careworn, the children fine strong, happy and healthy looking, large dark eyes and rosy cheeks, very pretty and intelligent looking both of them. Amy I should think would turn out to be a very handsome girl. Half an hour's walking took us to the house, a regular bushman's abode, small and compact, about 120 acres, 130 sheep. I feasted on dainties at his house – everything clean neat and tidy but all at the same time says "hard up, hard up". He has tried wheat, corn, cattle etc but nothing pays. Mrs Bigg is a pleasant woman, good figure and carriage and I should say a good disciplinarian to judge by the children who are very well-behaved without being shy. She has left me - or rather I have left her - with a great idea of her common sense and general usefulness, the very woman for a

12. *This looks a slight exaggeration - the official total rainfall for Armidale in 1872 was 33.6 inches, with only January and October being rather wet. Records from 1867 to May 1871 are missing but the last half year of 1871 resulted in 14.5 inches of rain. The downpour in Sydney could not have been that great as in the list of metropolitan rainfalls exceeding 10 inches in 24 hours, there was none for the years 1870 to 1873. (Source-Dr K Bigg.)*

Bushman's wife. At the same time I think she would have been equal to the occasion had fortune made her mistress of The Hyde. The children go off to school every morning, a mile and a half walk to Uralla. Alfred seems very fond of reading, each evening he took up a book. Amy and I played dominoes and draughts and we were capital friends. I quite lost my heart to Amy. They both seem very fond of their father and mother and they of them."

This is the principal part relating to Henry, most interesting to us. He stayed with them from Sunday to Wednesday and was very far from well, being knocked up with his journey. It was certainly kind of him to undertake it.

DIARY ENTRY IN JUNE 1873.

Henry gives us an account of Tom Donkin's visit. They liked him very much. They are having fine weather again, so the sheep are doing much better and he is now of "chaff cutting" for the mail contractor. That is, when he gets a machine which will cost him £50 – he hopes that may pay. He is so sorry to hear of the death of Edward's baby and speaks so much and so feelingly about it.[13]

DIARY ENTRY IN JULY 1873.

Henry says he is going into chaff cutting directly as he has at last got Mr Mail Contractor to get him a small second-hand cutter for £30 and he is going to pay him in degrees in *chaff. Then he is obliged to get £50 from the bank by giving a lien on his next clip of wool. How thankful he will be for some of the money which he will have heard of by this time and I hope he will have the £15. There was also a long letter from Annie, she still complains very much of her eyes. She wants a greatcoat for Alfred and some stuff for a riding habit for Amy.*

DIARY ENTRY IN AUGUST 1873.

Henry's letter was principally about Uncle Tite's death, he writes so nicely about it.[14] *Annie complains very much of her eyes so that she finds difficulty in writing. Amy's foot is quite well but in other respects things are not improving. At times Henry is very sanguine of success in his undertakings but they seldom seem to come to anything and she says they get more behindhand and now we have to mortgage their sheep. Neither had Henry heard anything of the two horses he lost. I think they must now have heard of the different sums of money coming to them which must put them in good spirits. Little boy is improving in his writing, says he is in the third class and Amy soon will be in the second, that his Papa has a chaff cutter and he caught his fingers in one of the cog wheels and his Papa tells him that his Uncle William (Henry's younger brother) did the same to his finger and tells us about the tin mines etc.*

13. *The baby was his brother's firstborn, Edward Devas Bigg. The tragic story of his brother's children is related in Chapter 5.*

14. *Sir William Tite left £350,000–a fortune in those times - with £150 of it coming to Henry. £350,000 would be the equivalent of £21.5M today, with Henry's share being worth £9,250.*

DIARY ENTRY IN SEPTEMBER 1873.

Henry had our letter telling him of Sir William Tite's death and says it was very kind of him to leave him a legacy and he need hardly say what a blessing the money will be to him when he gets it. I suppose he also has the £15 Augusta, William and I sent as he says he is quite overwhelmed by so much kindness and by this time he must have heard of Uncle John's £50. Annie has gone to Armidale taking Alfred to have an ugly front tooth out that disfigures him. His sheep are doing well now, he has 300 and as half of them are ewes he hopes to get a good increase after lambing in about two months which must be about now. Annie says the sheep are not doing well as they have had three weeks of such wet weather and they are very lame and she cannot say their affairs are improved since she last wrote, yet they have not had any fresh disasters and they are all in good health.

DIARY ENTRY IN OCTOBER 1873.

The first time Amy has written and she signs herself Augusta Emily. She tells me she has had a birthday party and five little girls came from Uralla and two from the lagoon. Alfred improves very much in his writing, he tells us he is going to school and is doing long division money and practice. They have also found the two horses they lost some time ago.

DIARY ENTRY IN NOVEMBER 1873.

Henry had not received his legacy but with his Uncle John's present he had bought 11 head of cattle for £20 and he is now laying down 7 acres for hay to make chaff of, also getting his paddock paled in sheep proof which will save the expense of a boy to mind them. They both write in good spirits. Their sheep were doing well and they really hope things have taken a turn for the better.

DIARY ENTRY IN DECEMBER 1873.

Henry wrote to his Aunt Tite and they had received the legacy and wrote in better spirits.

DIARY ENTRY IN JANUARY 1874.

Had very nice letters from Henry and Annie who wrote in better spirits. There had been less rain and the sheep in consequence were doing better. Henry speaks so highly of his children, says they are nice looking as well as good. Emily/Amy will be quite handsome and is such a splendid figure. She walks like a ballet girl or an actress. It distresses him very much that he is unable to send her to a good school, as she is inclined to be rude as well as hasty-tempered. Alfred is just the reverse, though he has great spirits, he is so gentlemanly, good tempered and well-behaved and although he would not say it to anyone else he thinks sometimes he is as near perfection as it is possible for a boy to be. Annie complains very much about her eyes and it is a sad thing that she cannot get some good advice.

DIARY ENTRY IN JANUARY 1874.

Yesterday I sent the Box off to Australia. It went up to Maynard and Harris 126 Leadenhall Street, who will send it to him at J. McCrossin in Uralla, New England.

DIARY ENTRY IN MARCH 1874.

Heard from Henry and also from his little girl who will be 10 in June. Henry had just got through the shearing and the wool fetched £59. The sheep are not doing as well as he could have wished and have increased but little but still they pay. He was also making hay and a heavy crop which he hopes will bring a good sum of money when converted into chaff but the weather was rainy as usual so he had great difficulty getting it in dry.

DIARY ENTRY IN MAY 1874.

Annie says diphtheria is raging in Armidale and it is just 10 years ago that her little Freddy died from that disease. She complains very much of her eye though she does not think it gets worse. There has been an agriculture and flower show there and it was a great success. Henry got a prize for sheep and their apples were highly commended. For the first time she speaks of the Tichborne case being over and they heard the result in six days.[15] *Alfred also writes and says he is learning geometry and practice he also sends his drawing book but that is a mistake as it did not come.*

DIARY ENTRY IN JUNE 1874.

Going on much as usual, frost every night and very cold. "The sheep had been washed, though too cold but others about us were having theirs done".

DIARY ENTRY IN AUGUST 1874.

Henry wishes us to send our letters in future via Suez. The chaff cutting is paying pretty well but he has spent as much money upon it (over £60). He gets a profit of about £2 per ton and sells about a ton and a quarter. He hopes to make a much larger report in the summer as he is growing his own hay and his sheep are doing pretty well but he thinks of selling them as he wants the money. He wants 10/- a piece for them. Annie also writes that she has been quite laid up and obliged to have a doctor, it was something the matter with her lungs and heart brought on by overwork. She was a little better. Little Emily sent a letter very nicely written. She was going to have a birthday party when she would be ten years old. They were expecting to hear of the Box that I had sent every day.

DIARY ENTRY IN SEPTEMBER 1874.

Annie is rather better but her side troubles her still, her eyes are stronger and general health improved. She says Uralla is getting quite an important place. When they went there 9 years ago there was no school nearer than Armidale 20 miles off. Now they are to have a reading room and debating class and Henry looks forward to it so much. The Box has been in Sydney six weeks and the delay is due to the Bill of Lading, or Waybill as Henry calls it which I sent to Mr McCrossin and I suppose he did not get it. Henry really thinks his business has taken a turn for the better and the chaff cutting is paying well and every prospect of increase and he had so much grass that if he got a good crop of hay it would be a small fortune in itself.

15. *The Tichborne case was followed throughout the English-speaking world. One Arthur Orton started proceedings to claim the Tichborne inheritance in 1871. He ended up being tried for perjury and was imprisoned until 1884.*

DIARY ENTRY IN DECEMBER 1874.

Henry is still troubled over money matters and Annie tells him it is a pity he should have such large ideas with such small means. She sends over some more photographs of the children. They both have very bad mouths.

(Aunt Spence, the diarist's sister, died in December 1874 and Robert Spence sent cheques of £450 as part payment under the terms of the will to Augusta, William and Frederick. Henry is not mentioned although the will says "all surviving nieces and nephews to share equally". There is little doubt, therefore, that a similar sum was sent to Henry in New England.)

DIARY ENTRY IN FEBRUARY 1875.

Henry says they are going to send Emily to a Boarding School which is about to open in Armidale. He has once more appealed to Aunt Tite, he hopes and trusts it may be the last time. He would not have done so now had he not considered it such an important case. The National School was doing her harm. He had written thus far when Aunt's letter came to hand with its glad tidings (a gift I believe of £200) "so now we will have no difficulty in paying for the schooling". He had just sent a letter to her which was so annoying but at all counts it will tell her how much he was in want of it and for what purpose. Also a letter from Annie, Alfred and Emily. Emily tells us that she is going to school at Armidale after Christmas and the lady has five such nice little girls. She does not know how she will like to leave Mama and Papa for such a long time. She is going to learn music, singing and drawing.

DIARY ENTRY ABOUT A LETTER DATED 11TH FEB 1875.

Amy has been at school three weeks and they miss her so much. Henry's hay was a great success this year he had a very heavy crop and fine weather to get it up – it is oaten hay. He had a splendid crop of wheat 7ft. high but he is cutting it into chaff as he gets a good price for it. Annie has managed to sew her finger in the sewing machine which was very painful as the needle went right through the end of the forefinger, thread as well and he had some trouble drawing it out.

DIARY ENTRY IN MAY 1875.

Henry cannot get over Amy's loss, much as they had prayed to God to give her the means for educating her. They are pleased with the lady that Amy is with and she speaks very well of the child, says she is amiable and sweet-tempered and they are all very fond of her. Not so quick in some things as she could wish but she does her best and is sure to get on. Annie says she is feeling better than she has done for years and her eyes are much stronger. She finds the sewing machine a great help and they can keep a girl now, so she is able to go out more. Alfred likes her to go to meet him every evening.

Like his father (Smith Henry), Henry was not successful in business ventures. This may be accounted for by a family anecdote that goes back to the time of the Crusades. Apparently a certain character by the name of Bigg stole a Priest's chalice somewhere in France. The Priest hotly pursued him down the street shouting curses that each (successive) father would lose his money and the son would have to start over again. It was obviously a powerful curse!

How like his father Henry seems to have been. Annie probably put her finger on it when she remarked that it was a pity he should have such large ideas with such little means. It seems that every letter from Annie and Henry finding its way to Swallowfield in West Sussex reversed the last report. If one letter reported gloom and despair, the next said things were a little better, only for the following one to report calamity and so on. But the underlying story was one of a family desperately trying to make ends meet. Almost all the time their fortunes (if that is the right expression) seemed to have been at the whim of the climate, being beset with times of drought on the one hand and constant rain and storms at other times. It must have been a rough and punishing existence.

No doubt there were many times when Henry and Annie sat down late into the evening wondering how they could ever pull themselves out of debt and put their financial affairs on a healthy footing. We have read how Henry was always dreaming up new ways to earn money for the hard-pressed family. How many different jobs and trades did he try his hand at? In the previous pages there are eleven ventures recorded - droving sheep, fruit growing, raising cattle, keeping horses, growing produce for re-sale, melon growing, raising sheep, arable farming, prospecting for tin, the carrying trade with dray horses and a wagon and chaff cutting! We can surmise that there were many other schemes that passed through his head, besides these, with Annie at her wits' end to prevent him charging off into some new enterprise. Unfortunately, it seems as though every new bright idea for making money needed an investment to start with. And as soon as money was made or received it was used to pay off a debt for the previous failed scheme, or immediately spent in speculating into a new one. We can be sure, however, that Annie would have been fiercely proud of Henry and his repeated efforts to earn a living for the family. In truth, many pioneer families in Australia were faced with these problems and challenges.

The only true hope Henry and Annie had of getting themselves out of debt was by coming into some of the family money, and it must have been the hope of this that kept them going. After all, it was not altogether an unlikely prospect. There was money in the Bigg (and Tite/Curtis) family, and some of the relatives who were comfortably off were unmarried, without issue, single and very elderly. And no doubt the letters sent home to Smith Henry and Augusta would be talked about amongst the family, and so their dire straits would be known.

In terms of gifts we have seen that relatives did respond to the news of their problems in Australia. Unsolicited gifts of money were sent at various times, and on the occasions Henry found it necessary to ask for help it was generously given. In all probability Henry and Annie would have had to sell up to pay off their indebtedness if these kind donations had not been forthcoming.

As has already been mentioned, Henry did not inherit The Hyde when his Uncle Edward who owned it died in 1871, although he must have had every expectation of it passing to him as the eldest of Smith Henry's sons. The property went instead to his younger brother Edward, with the proviso that Lucy should be allowed to reside there for as long as it pleased her to do so. That was the biggest opportunity to inherit money that he could have contemplated, and despite his comments at the time, he must have secretly rued his continuing misfortune on learning that he had been passed over.

Still, Henry's salvation was on hand, and it was by way of an inheritance that he was lifted from the poverty of their existence in New England. On 17th May 1875, Henry's Great Aunt Lucy sent a letter to his father (Smith Henry) saying that she would be dead before he read it. Augusta and Smith Henry at home at Swallowfield had heard this line so many times that they discounted it. But this time it was to be true; on 18th May Aunt Lucy, aged 77, was found dead in the waters of one of the beautiful lakes in the grounds of The Hyde where she lived. Because she had forecast her immediate demise there was great fear in the family that the Coroner would pronounce a verdict of suicide, or that she would be found to have been temporarily insane. Thankfully for all concerned the result of the inquest was that she was "found drowned, no evidence to show how she came into the water".

Her will provided for all her property to be left to her brother, Smith Henry Bigg, for life, and after that it was to be divided amongst his five children. As Augusta records it in her diary- "Our children now come into the property which belonged to Misses Bigg and Edward Bigg". Smith Henry inherited just under £10,000 from Lucy - in the order of £625,000 in today's terms (1999).

What transpired next is unclear. Maybe Smith Henry decided to pass down some of his new-found wealth to his oldest son and for this reason called him to come to England and see him. (After all, one fifth of what was left of Lucy's money would eventually pass down to Henry when his father died, if the estate was equally divided amongst his children.) Perhaps Smith Henry decided to pass on some of this future entitlement of his inheritance to Henry a little earlier. Perhaps Henry just decided on his own initiative to return home to see his parents, we may never know.

In any event, Henry and his wife and two young children (Amy and Alfred) took passage to England to meet his parents at Swallowfield in Mannings Heath, Sussex in March 1876. What a homecoming that must have been after 20 years away. Henry would have then been 41 years old. His sister Augusta who was only 20 when he had left for Australia was now 40 years old; his brother William was now 34 and the "youngster", Frederick, now 29. I wonder if Henry asked after the pigeons he had left in William's care! The visit lasted six months, and after celebrating Christmas together, Henry and his family sailed home on the "Durham" from Gravesend in January the following year, arriving at Melbourne, Australia in March 1877. (See Annex B.)

There can be absolutely no doubt that some financial arrangement had been reached between father and the eldest son during the visit, as Henry returned back to New England a reasonably wealthy man. For the time being, at least, Henry was in that position which he and Annie had dreamed of during those dreadfully hard years at Uralla. They were now out of debt, had funds at their disposal, and could look forward to a new future.

Soon after his return to Australia, between July 1878 and September 1878, Henry sold his small estate at Uralla and acquired a large tract of land on either side of the Gara River, about 6 to 12 miles north-east of Armidale, New South Wales. No more 40 acre blocks for Henry and Annie now, and so much for Smith Henry's 90 acres at Swallowfield and Edward's 1,000 acres at The Hyde. Henry purchased 23,000 acres from Fraser and Anderson bordering each side of the Gara from below Herbert Park to just north of the homestead known as Brookside, well below that homestead on the western side of the river across to the Burying Ground Creek and up on to the Herbert Park Road, leaving out a property owned by the Maguires called Eastview. He called his new property "Thalgarrah", where a very substantial house for the times was built (See Map page 142).

Although it enclosed over 20,000 acres, he only owned 1/3rd of it outright, as it contained "selections" owned by Nelson, Allingham, Mitchell and McCully. Selections arose as a result of the Robertson Land Bill of 1861. This gave anyone the right to select and purchase on freehold title (at a cost of £1 per acre) any land that had not been surveyed by a Government surveyor – even if that land was held on lease by an original selector. However, the freehold purchaser was required to reside on his selection, fence it or do improvements to the value of £40. This was a considerable sum in those days and seldom complied with. These selections caused Henry no end of trouble when he tried to buy them out. He was eventually successful, but only after protracted negotiations and acrimonious dispute. In East Paddock James Mitchell owned 11 acres of selected land, on the flat in front of the house running from the river back into the scrub, where he had built his hut. William Allingham owned 40 acres on the Brookside boundary. Both were good cultivation blocks with permanent water and both men were reluctant to sell out. Sometimes an independent arbitrator was required to see a fair price for the selector's improvements. For example: "*Walter valued the improvements at £350*". *Henry offered him £200.* "*I do not suppose he will sell and be dammed to him*", Henry wrote angrily at one time. Later Lewis wanted £500 for it.

Unfortunately, Henry had quite a vendetta going against these selectors in order to get his way and we see another side of him for the first time. Apparently at one time he threw one of their ploughs into the river, complete with harness. On another occasion he let their horses out, and even went so far as to take the bark cladding off Allingham's hut on the pretext it had been empty so long he no longer needed it.

Eventually after complicated exchanges of reserves and freehold it was all under one ownership, but only after the boundaries had contracted and most of the remainder was mortgaged to the Bank of New South Wales.

The family had moved from Uralla to a hut on the banks of the Gara River beside a ford on the Rockville Road, where the acacia trees still stood a hundred years later. This move was temporary whilst Messrs. Williams, Seabrook and Brown were engaged (in 1878) to construct a brick house with a shingle (later upgraded to a slate) roof. A shearing shed of 8 stands, stables and forge and other buildings were also to be constructed. The trouble with the temporary accommodation was that when the river rose, people and animals camped near to them, so a new site was chosen on a rise above a lake, set well back from the road.

Henry reconstructed part of England in a beautiful orchard on his new station between lake and river, with many fruit trees (apples, pomegranate, medlar, mulberry). He also planted willows, poplars, elms, conifers, rose gardens etc. In its prime it was apparently a wonderful place, particularly for the children, and even fifty years later it was still beautiful. (Sadly, during the 1939–45 war and afterwards it was neglected; but the autumn colours of the English trees that remain are still a sight to behold to this day.)

Always with the idea of being self-sufficient, in addition to the fruit trees he planted grape vines, berries and kept bees. A story survives that he sacked a gardener for failing to water the valuable blackberry vines he had imported. Later, the vines were to spread over half of New England and provide wonderful cover for that other import – the rabbit!

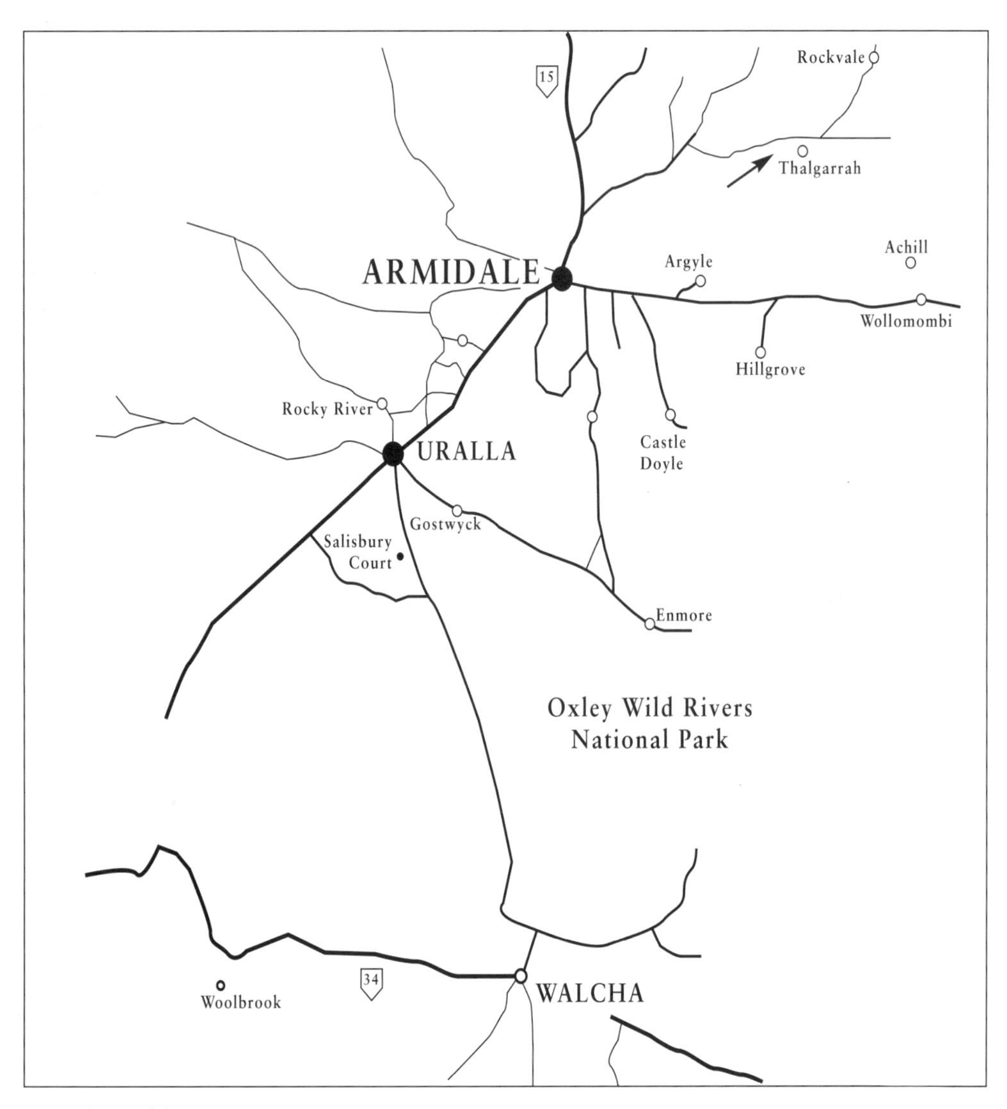

Map of Armidale area

In 1885 a new neighbour arrived on the scene. Henry's first cousin once removed, Henry Welch Curtis, arrived from England set on gaining experience from Henry. He was the eldest son of Frederick Thomas Curtis, Solicitor, and his second wife Mary Sicard Delmar, of Dry Hills Park, Tonbridge in Kent. He started work for Henry as Bookkeeper on the Thalgarrah estate, with Henry reporting: "*Henry [Curtis] is doing well. I am very pleased with him. Among other ideas he has got a new ledger with Index and is keeping accounts with extreme neatness*".[16] The following year Henry Bigg wrote: "*Henry is going on well, he is inclined to argue occasionally and to think he knows more than me – but only occasionally*".

Henry Curtis landed on his feet, as they say in the new country. Three years after arriving he bought 12,000 acres on the eastern side of the river opposite Herbert Park, bordering on Henry and Annie's property. He had also proposed marriage to Henry and Annie's daughter Amy (Augusta Emily). Henry Curtis was her second cousin. They were married on 11th July 1888, a little after Amy's 24th birthday.

Amy and her new husband were given a generous wedding present by her parents - two paddocks comprising some 500 acres from the Thalgarrah property to attach to their own 12,000 acres. They called their property and the house they built on it "Brooklyn".

They had three daughters and two sons, who were the progenitors of the Curtis family in Australia. We will come across the Curtises many times altogether in our story.

(Incidentally, Henry Welch Curtis' brother, Arthur Sicard Curtis, also emigrated to Australia - and married Lucy Burraston, a cousin of Amy's. They had two daughters. The two Curtis brothers, Henry and Arthur were said to have been sent to Australia because they were "naughty boys", which perhaps meant they were in some sort of mischief at home, so perhaps transportation was still going on in one form or another even at this late date.)

There was another wedding in the family only two years after Henry and Amy's marriage. On 16th April 1890 Henry and Annie's son, Alfred, Amy's brother, married Mabel Emily Spasshatt, daughter of the late Dr. S.P. Spasshatt and his wife Angela Spasshatt nee Nixon, at St. Peter's Anglican Cathedral, Armidale. Mabel was the youngest of Dr and Mrs Spasshatt's four daughters, and her father had been one of the first doctors practising in Armidale. He had died quite suddenly from typhoid fever when Mabel was little more than a baby, and his widow had been left to support herself and four girls under the age of 9.[17]

The amusing story of how Alfred and Mabel became engaged has been passed down through the family and goes something like this. In those times the hopeful bridegroom had to go along to his girl's parents and ask for their daughter's hand in marriage. But Alfred managed to pick a bad day, because Mabel was away from home staying with the Belfield family at "Eversleigh". There were no telephones in those days, so a

16. One of these ledgers was rescued from a heap of decaying rubbish in the sheds behind Thalgarrah around 1945 and has been added to the family records.

17. Angela "Nina" Spasshatt supported her children by becoming a schoolteacher and opening a school. She is remembered by some members of the family for the way she used a ruler during piano lessons. Not to conduct, or to tap out time, but to reward a bad note with a rap over the knuckles!

message had to be sent to Mabel informing her that Alfred had asked for her hand. There are two versions of how the message was sent and what it said. One account has it that Mabel received a telegram saying "COME HOME MABEL YOU ARE TO BE MARRIED", whereas the other mentions a short note being sent from her widowed Mother along the lines "Mabel, you must make arrangements to come home at once, you are engaged to be married". Either way, the crucial piece of information - who Mabel was going to marry - seems to have been missed out, and Mabel had to wait until she returned home to find out.

They had two daughters and four sons who were to become the progenitors of the Bigg family in Australia, whom we will also come across later in our story. The newly married couple spent their honeymoon in New Zealand and then returned to the new home that had been built for them on the East Paddock of the Thalgarrah property - which they called "Swallowfield", after the family home back in Sussex.

(So now our book has two Swallowfields to contend with. To avoid any confusion, from here on the UK Swallowfield will simply be referred to by that name, whereas the property in Australia will be referred to as Swallowfield NSW.)

But before we pass on to further generations we have to finish Henry's Story. So what happened to Henry and Annie after their children married? Thalgarrah was not a large station by the standards in that area, but still substantial enough to require much hard work and effort to run properly.

In 1897 Henry gave about half an acre of land adjoining the Rockvale Road, near the gate to the homestead, for a church to be built. In due time a wooden church was built on the site and dedicated as All Saints, Church of England, part of the Parish of Hillgrove, in the Diocese of Armidale and Grafton. Within 30 years it had been destroyed by white ants and was replaced by a church of brick construction.

Henry worked the estate with Alfred until he was tragically killed as a result of an accident in the saddle at the age of 68. Apparently his horse wheeled under the limb of a tree as he was rounding up cattle and he was knocked heavily to the ground. He developed pneumonia and died shortly afterwards, on 25th September 1902. So our Little Henry who had been sent to Australia because of his weak chest spent some 46 years of his life in tough conditions, toiling as a pioneer in the early years to support his young family.

Henry's will was brief. He left everything to his son, Alfred, on condition that his widow, Annie, would have use of Thalgarrah and its contents for her life, as well as £200 per annum. His estate was worth £10,111 net.

Annie lived on at Thalgarrah for a further 8 years, until her death on 1st February 1911 after a short illness, whilst staying with her eldest grandson, Fred Curtis at Abbey Green, Guyra. She was 70 years old. Annie was buried in Armidale cemetery beside her dear Henry.

With the death of Henry and his wife this chapter closes and we now move on to the second eldest child of Smith Henry and Augusta Bigg, their daughter Augusta, to see what happened in her life.

Henry Bigg, eldest son of Smith Henry and Augusta Bigg who left West Sussex for New South Wales at the age of 22.

However, we will return to pick up the threads of Alfred and Amy's stories and that of their properties at Brooklyn and Swallowfield NSW, as well as the Thalgarrah station, in a later chapter.

Of all the fourteen children of the two people we started off our story with (ie Edward Bigg b.1760 and his wife Sarah) only one son, Smith Henry Bigg, had a son who was to continue this Bigg line. This son, Henry Edward Bigg, who has been the subject of this chapter himself had only one surviving son to carry on the Bigg line, but not in England. Henry's son, Alfred, was first–generation Australian.

Lady Emily Tite, nee Curtis, sister of Smith Henry's wife Augusta. Her husband, Sir William Tite, died in 1873 leaving Henry an inheritance that was sorely needed.

Anne ("Annie") Bigg, nee Burraston who married Henry in 1860.

The lagoon and the old racecourse circuit that ringed it in Henry's day, near Uralla. Henry and his family had a 40 acre block of land adjacent to the lagoon and racecourse in 1865. *Photo – Tony Turner*

Chapter Four
Augusta's Story

Augusta, the only daughter of Smith Henry and his wife (also Augusta), lived for the rest of her life in Mannings Heath after moving there with her parents in 1845; most of the time she lived at Swallowfield with her parents while they still lived, and for a time with her brothers.

First to leave home was not her oldest brother Henry, but William, who went off to Tonbridge School for his education in 1852. He came back for the school holidays, but Augusta missed his company deeply. Four years later came Henry's sudden departure for Australia, so then the parents shared the large house and its beautiful estate with Augusta, and her three younger brothers, Edward, William and Frederick.

Augusta remained unmarried, and was the classic dutiful daughter of that period. As a younger woman living at Swallowfield with her parents she was often called upon to act as companion to her various aunts when they wished to "take the waters" at one of the many spas that were fashionable in England at the time. She also accompanied them when they journeyed to recuperate at such seaside resorts as Folkestone and Ramsgate on the South Coast.

Her much-loved brother William returned home from India ill with disease in 1871 at the age of 29 and was nursed by his mother and sister at Swallowfield for the next ten years. He died at Swallowfield before reaching his 40th birthday. Augusta was heartbroken by William's death. In the same year he died she commissioned the building of a small church in Mannings Heath, along the road that runs through the village now appropriately named Church Road.

Known locally in the early days as the Mission Church, but properly from the outset as The Church of the Good Shepherd, this memorial to her brother was consecrated in December 1881. There are two memorial plaques in the church to record its erection and dedication.

The first consists of a stained-glass window in the chancel, on the side-wall of the church, under which is a brass plaque bearing the inscription-

"To the Glory of God
and in loving memory of
William Bigg
This building was erected
By his sister
October 26th 1881"

The second plaque, positioned to the right of the altar rail, reads-

"Church of the Good Shepherd
To the Glory of God
And for the services of the
Church of England.
Dedicated December 6th 1881
In loving memory of William Bigg
this building was erected by his sister
October 26th 1881"

The large two-piece stained-glass window behind the altar in the Mission Church carries the legend-

"To the Glory of God and to the memory of their beloved parents Smith Henry and Augusta Bigg this window is dedicated by their children"

Augusta was ever mindful of her own religious duties and kept a caring and watchful eye on the well-being and spiritual life of the family, extending that interest in later years as far as the Antipodes.

She is remembered in Mannings Heath for her interest in church matters. As well as gifting the little church to the parish, in 1894 she also provided a house in the parish for the curate to occupy. (Identified as the Presbytery, this house is situated on the main road, the A281, that runs past Mannings Heath from Horsham and on to Monk's Gate and Cowfold to the south. It is today called Hazelwood. It was sold in the 1980s and the proceeds provide a source of continuing income to the parish to this day. (See map in Chapter 9).

Her father, Smith Henry, lived to the age of 83 and passed away at Swallowfield in 1885, when Augusta was 50.

Augusta inherited half of Swallowfield when her mother died in 1888, the other half of the estate going to Edward Francis, her brother. Her mother's will provided that she should be allowed to live at Swallowfield during her lifetime.

In due course, however, Augusta moved out of Swallowfield and took up residence in a home of her own called Ryecroft, which was also situated in the village at Mannings Heath. (Ryecroft and the land that surrounded it was sold for development in the 1980s, and is now an estate of some 34 houses, called Whytings.)

She attended the Church of the Good Shepherd until well into her eighties, being transported there in a wicker bath chair pulled by one of her gardeners and accompanied by two of her maids. She died in 1922 and is buried in the family grave at St. Andrew's Parish Church, Nuthurst.

Augusta's death is commemorated in the Church of the Good Shepherd by the installation of finely carved wooden altar rails to replace the original iron altar rails.

A brass plaque alongside this tribute to such a generous benefactor to the village, reads -

"To the Glory of God
and in memory of
Augusta Bigg
At Rest January 14th 1922"

Augusta was a very wealthy spinster when she died, having inherited property and possessions from her parents. In addition to owning the Ryecroft property, she had a share and interest in what was called the "Family Settlement", which was known to include 8 houses in Edgware Road, London, 3 houses in Thwaites Place, Edgware Road and 2 houses in Marylebone Road, London. She made a will in November 1913 when she was 78 years old carefully setting out what she wished to happen to her estate. But the advent of the Great War soon after led to depreciation in the value of some of her securities, and as a consequence, she made a codicil to her will in July 1915 reducing some of the legacies, allowances and annuities. Then, following the death of one of her nominated executors and trustees she entered into a second codicil, in 1916, which also caused some further adjustment. A summary of the will insofar as it may be of interest to readers of this book is given below. (NB This is not a complete summary.)

Beneficiary	Relationship	Amount	Adjusted Amount	Comments
Frederick Bigg	Brother	£500 and the small painting of old Nuthurst church by Miss Symes.		
Rose Bigg	Sister-in-law, wife of Frederick	£1,000 and the Davenport formerly in the Dining Room. Also a gold necklet and the Prayer Book from the poor people of Nuthurst.		Also 1/2 of remainder of household furniture and effects, plated goods, watches, jewels, trinkets, etc
Fanny Bigg	Sister-in-law, wife of Edward Francis	£1,000 and £200 pa.	£200 pa annuity to £100 pa	Also 1/2 of remainder of household furniture and effects, plated goods, watches, jewels, trinkets, etc
Alfred Edward Bigg	Nephew, son of late Henry Edward	£1,000. Also the family plate engraved with the crest "the Martlet" left by late mother to Frederick off whom she purchased it. And 1/2 residue of the estate in trust.		
Mabel Bigg	Wife of Alfred Edward	£500		

Beneficiary	Relationship	Amount	Adjusted Amount	Comments
Edward Arthur Bigg	Cousin	£25		
Augusta Emily Curtis	Niece, daughter of late brother Henry Edward,.....	£1,000 and 1/2 of residence. Also, plate, gold watch, chain and bracelet, set of gold earrings and brooch given by Sir W Tite. And 1/2 residue of estate in trust.		Residence would be Ryecroft. (The £1,000 was to be reduced by any amount unpaid of the loan Augusta had previously made to Henry Edward.)
	... and Godchild	£300	£300 to £100	
William Spasshatt Bigg	Godchild	£300	£300 to £100	
Dr Mark Vernon	Friend and medical attendant	£100	£100 to £50	
Anne Moulding	Servant	£20 as a servant and 1 year's wages. Also the income from £700 held in trust for her.	£700 in trust increased to £900	
Richard Weller	Coachman	£20		At The Hyde
Ambrose Langridge	Gardener	£10		At The Hyde
Mark Ashby	Keeper	£10		At The Hyde
Mary Anne Raby	Maid	£20		At The Hyde
Emily Tullett	Former servant	£20		
Helen Tullett	Former servant	£10		
Revd. L Robinson		£10		Of Devon Lodge, Monks Gate
Church of the Good Shepherd		£2,500	£2,500 to £2,000	In trust for maintenance and support of the church.
Horsham Cottage Hospital		£100	£100 to £50	
Bishop of Chichester's Fund		£200	£100 to £50	
Clergy Pensions Institute		£100	£100 to £50	
Corp of Sons of the Clergy		£100	£100 to £50	
The Church Army		£100	£100 to £50	
William Reading	Schoolmaster	£26pa		Mannings Heath
Each domestic servant, incl. Coachman		£20 each, plus any wages owing	The £20 to Coachman Herbert Rushton was revoked in the second codicil (he had died!)	Provided they were in employment with Augusta at her death and had been in service for a year or more.

The principal beneficiaries were clearly her late brother Henry's children Alfred and Augusta Emily, known as Amy, living in Australia. In 1922 when Augusta died Alfred would have been 59 and Amy 57.

Augusta Bigg, only daughter of Smith Henry and Augusta Bigg.

Interior of the Church of The Church of the Good Shepherd around 1932. *Photo - Allen Flint*

The Church of The Good Shepherd in 1999. *Photo - Tony Turner*

Joy and Cecil Curtis paying a visit to Augusta's second home, Ryecroft, in Mannings Heath in 1975. Ryecroft no longer exists, having been pulled down and developed as the Whytings estate in 1984. - *Photo - Joy Curtis*

Chapter Five
Edward's Story

Edward Francis, the third child of Smith Henry and Augusta, was born on 9th April 1837 at Hampstead, London, and moved to Swallowfield with the family when he was 8 years old. He lived there until he was 28, when he married Fanny, the only daughter of the late William Everington Esq. Fanny was 19 years old when she married Edward at Lambeth in London.

Following in the footsteps of his uncle (Edward), he qualified as a barrister.

As we have heard in earlier chapters, Edward's uncle, Edward Smith Bigg Esq., a Justice of the Peace, owned a large country house and estate about 3 km from Mannings Heath called The Hyde. This uncle had never married and lived at The Hyde with his three spinster sisters, Sarah, Ellen and Lucy. By the time his uncle Edward died in 1871, Sarah and Ellen had also passed away, both in the same year, 1865.

As recounted in Chapter 3 Henry's Story, Edward Smith Bigg did not leave The Hyde to his brother, Smith Henry Bigg, or to the older nephew, Henry, who was then in Australia, but to Henry's younger brother, Edward Francis. (There was a proviso that Lucy should be permitted to continue living at The Hyde for the rest of her life. Lucy died in one of the lakes at the Hyde in 1875.)

The Hyde was, and still is to this day, a large country house set in beautiful gardens, with lakes (hammer ponds), surrounded by woodland and farmland estate. It is extensive, covering almost 1,000 acres. Edward and Fanny would have been astounded at their good fortune in inheriting such a wonderful property. They must have marvelled at their luck. But within five years of moving in to The Hyde they were burdened with terrible tragedy.

First, in February 1873, their new-born baby son, Edward Devas Bigg, died at a little over 3 months of age. Edward and Fanny, heartbroken at their loss, resolved to try again for the family they so desperately wanted and very shortly Fanny became pregnant for the second time. On 21 January 1874 she gave birth to another son, only to see him pass away within 10 minutes of being born. These two setbacks would have been difficult enough for any couple to cope with, but yet again they tried for the children they yearned for. Within a few short months Fanny was again with child, and Edward's family and the Everington family and their friends prayed for them to be blessed with a healthy child this time. Fanny went into labour for the third time at Grosvenor Hill, Wimbledon on the 7th February 1875 and gave birth to a daughter who they named Evelyn Fanny.

However, Edward and Fanny's personal tragedies were by no means over. Elation at the birth of their new offspring lasted but a few, short months, and by June of the same year, little Evelyn had passed away at her parents' home at The Hyde.

Three times now Edward and Fanny had been in despair, seeing their young babies taken from them. Each individual loss must have been heartbreaking; to endure three such occurrences is beyond our comprehension.

By the Autumn of 1875 Fanny became pregnant for the fourth time. As with her other births, Fanny decided to have her baby at Grosvenor Hill, Wimbledon. Would fate curse them again, or would she be blessed with a healthy baby this time? Family and friends once again went through the process of praying and hoping, and supporting Fanny in every way possible.

On 16th June 1876 Fanny gave birth to another daughter, Helen Mary - and this baby survived. How thankful and delighted everyone must have been at the news. How relieved Fanny and Edward must have been; at long last a daughter safely delivered to them.

It would have been wonderful to have continued our story of Edward revealing how baby Helen had grown up to lead a happy life, cared for, watched over and loved by her devoted parents. But sadly, tragedy was only biding its time and would come again to strike this poor couple.

Helen died at Merton House, Wood Park, Dulwich before reaching her fourth birthday.

Until this narrative about the Bigg family was started it had been understood that the children had all been the victims of lead poisoning, having taken their water supply from the well at The Hyde, or from water supplied to the house through lead pipework. This is a plausible proposition because the water in the Horsham area was known to be of poor quality. There was no public supply of piped, clean water at this time, and inhabitants either took their needs from reservoirs fed from local rivers, or more often from a well sunk close to their property. Horsham's water invariably had a greasy film on the surface of it, and smelt dreadfully when heated. Although the Public Health Act of 1848 had promoted the provision of pure water and the treatment of sewage throughout the land, and The Local Government Act ten years later had endorsed the idea, in 1859 Horsham rejected the proposal to adopt the Acts by 160 votes to 6. Three years later an outbreak of scarlet fever hit the town severely, but still nothing was done. In 1865 a survey of Horsham's well water was carried out which showed that its water had 49 grains of impurity to every gallon, compared to Glasgow's 2 grains per gallon.

The Certificates of Death for the children, however, show that they all died of different causes, and poor water was not mentioned.

Four years later, Edward and Fanny dedicated a memorial to their children at the parish church of St. Mary, Slaugham, just a short distance from the estate. The memorial takes the form of two stained-glass windows, which are inscribed-

To the Glory of God and in loving memory of Edward Devas,
Evelyn Fanny and Helen Mary dear children of Edward and
Fanny Bigg. 1880.
Glory to God in the Highest and on Earth Peace

Understandably, Edward and Fanny were inconsolable over the loss of all their children and devoted the rest of their lives to running The Hyde and improving it, supporting their local church and doing good works in the community. They also extended generous hospitality to many of their relatives from far afield on occasions when they visited England. Edward continued to practise in the Law and was called to the Bar at the Inner Temple in London in 1883, joining the Western Circuit.

Edward died on 14th June 1907 at The Hyde, aged 70. His wife Fanny survived him for a period of 15 years, continuing to take great interest in church activities at Handcross.

The Mission Room at Handcross had been dedicated in 1876; before this divine services had been held in a room at the nearby "Red Lion" public house, with Sunday School being held in the old shop opposite. In the year of her husband's death a sanctuary was added to the Mission Room, thanks to Fanny's generosity. And again in 1915 it was chiefly due to Fanny's kindness that the Mission Room at Handcross was turned into a beautiful little church, following the completion of the Parish Hall.

Fanny Bigg passed away on 13th March 1922, just two months after Augusta Bigg, her sister-in-law, died at Ryecroft. Edward and Fanny are both buried in the churchyard at St. Mary's in Slaugham, and there is a brass memorial plaque to their memory immediately below the childrens' stained glass window. The east window at Handcross (built by Powell & Co) was a memorial to Fanny given by her blood relatives, the Etherington family.

After Fanny's death, The Hyde was sold out of the family to Colonel J.R. Warren and his wife, who owned the even larger estate adjacent to The Hyde called Handcross Park. (News of what has happened to The Hyde can be found in Chapter 8.) With no children to pass on her estate to most of Fanny's wealth passed to her (the Everington) side of the family. Again some of the beneficiaries will be of interest and are listed below. (NB This is not a complete summary.)

Beneficiary	Relationship	Amount	Comments
Edward Arthur Bigg	Executor	£100	Of Clifton, Bristol.
Rose Bigg	Wife of brother-in-law Frederick	£300	
Helen Rose Conway	Cousin	£25	See Miss Conway's letter in Chapter 8.
Alfred Edward Bigg	Late husband's nephew	£50	
Mabel Bigg	Wife of Alfred	£50	
Emily Augusta Bigg	Late husband's niece	£50	i.e Amy
Edward Lionel Bigg	Godson and son of Alfred and Mabel	£25	
Mary Ann Raby	"my faithful maid"	£200	
Elizabeth Raby	Housemaid.	£100	

Beneficiary	Relationship	Amount	Comments
Ada Webb	Widow of Charles Webb	£10	Probably Charles had been a servant
Annie Weller	Widow of late Coachman Richard Weller.	£5	
Ambrose Langridge	Gardener.	£100	
Emily Ashby	Widow of late Gamekeeper Mark Ashby	£25	
All Fanny's other domestic servants in service at her death		£10	Provided they had been in service for a year or more.

St. Mary's Church, Slaugham where Edward, his wife Fanny and their babies are buried. The children are remembered by a stained-glass memorial window. *Photo - Tony Turner*

Edward Francis Bigg, second son of Smith Henry and Augusta Bigg. He inherited The Hyde in 1871 upon the death of his Uncle.

Chapter Six
William's Story

William's story is short for a number of reasons. Of course, the principal one is that he died at the early age of 39, but the other reason is that he spent much of his career in the Army serving in India where little is known of his life and exploits.

Born on 26th October 1841 at Hampstead, William lived at Swallowfield from the age of 4 and grew up with Augusta and his brothers until they were separated when he was 11. At that age he went off to Tonbridge School for 6 years for his education.

What he did when his schooling was finished we know not, but four years later he joined the 63rd Foot Regiment via a commission bought for him by his parents. They could only afford a 2nd Lieutenant's commission, and only that after great difficulty. Why he entered the Army we do not know. Perhaps he had been attracted by the parades of soldiers that he saw in Horsham from time to time in his youth. The Army had been present in and around Horsham since the 18th century. Horsham Barracks were built on 12 acres of leased land in 1796 and over the next 18 years some 69 regiments were stationed there.

William may have been with his mother when she walked into town (Horsham) on 29th May 1845 and saw a regiment of soldiers on the way to Chichester. Augusta recorded the event in her diary, commenting *"The Regiment, the Buffs, had been in India for 23 years and out of 600 who left England only two have returned"*.

In considering how it was that young William became attracted to the Army, we have to take account of the events of the times. Probably his formative years for deciding what he wanted to do with his life would have been between, say, 7 and 15, that is between 1848 and 1856. Let us examine what was happening during that period in the British Empire to excite a young boy's mind:-

1848 - Boer War

- Battle of Boomplaatz: Boers defeated by Sir Harry Smith, governor of the Cape of Good Hope. Orange Free State proclaimed British Territory.

1848 - Second Sikh War

- Outbreak of the war in India between the British and the Sikhs: Punjab annexed.
- Battle of Kineyri: Sikhs defeated and fled to Multan.
- Battle of Suddasain: Sikh attack on British-led forces defeated.
- Siege of Multan: Attack on Multan by British forces began.

1849 - Second Sikh War

- Siege of Multan: City stormed and surrendered to British.
- Battle of Chilianwala: British and Indian troops defeat the Sikhs.
- Battle of Gujerat: British and Indian troops again crush Sikhs.
- Battle of Ramnuggur: British attempt to dislodge Sikh army unsuccessful.

1852 - Far East

- Annexation of Lower Burma by Britain.

1853 - Africa

- David Livingstone discovered the Victoria Falls.

1854 - Greece

- British and French troops occupy the Piraeus.

- Crimean War

- British and French troops land in the Crimea.
- Battle of the Alma: Russians defeated.
- Seige of Sebastopol began.
- Battle of Balaklava: Result indecisive.
- Charge of the Light Brigade.
- Battle of Inkerman: Russians defeated.

1855 - Crimean War

- Death of Lord Raglan.
- Battle of the Great Redan: Unsuccessful British attack on defences of Sebastopol.
- Siege of Sebastopol: Ended with seizure of city.

Perhaps this answers our question. This was exciting and attractive stuff to a young man of the times. Colourful adventures in overseas lands fighting the Queen's enemies and building an Empire, what more could a youngster yearn for than to enlist and wear the scarlet uniform. The Army was regarded as a fine career. Well, that is what William did, like so many young gentlemen of his time.

His career in the Army progressed well, and he was promoted to the rank of Captain in 1869. He spent some time in India, but as we have already heard in Augusta's story, he there became ill and was retired in 1871, keeping his rank as Captain.

Returning to Swallowfield, William continued to suffer ill heath for many years and was nursed lovingly by his Mother and Father, sister Augusta and Edward and Frederick until he died on 12th May 1881. He is buried in the family grave in the churchyard at St. Andrew's, Nuthurst.

Four years later his father, Smith Henry Bigg, died at the age of 83 and was buried in the grave of his son. Two and a half years later, his mother Augusta also died and was buried alongside Smith Henry and William.

The Bigg graves are located on the left side of the path leading from the lychgate past the church. (See diagram at the end of this chapter).

William Bigg in his youth.

William Bigg in uniform. - He joined the 63rd Foot Regiment as a 2nd Lieutenant, and later became a Captain.

William, probably close to the end of his short life.

There are four graves in a group at St. Andrew's, Nuthurst. On the left is a flat tomb bearing a large cross, inscribed on the top

- "WILLIAM BIGG FORMERLY A CAPTAIN IN HER MAJESTY'S 63rd REGIMENT BORN 26TH OCTOBER 1841 DIED 12th MAY 1881". At the foot of the tomb is inscribed- " SMITH HENRY BIGG OF SWALLOWFIELD IN THIS PARISH BORN MARCH 13th 1802 DIED NOVEMBER 22nd 1885". Along one side of the tomb is the inscription- "AUGUSTA BIGG WIFE OF SMITH HENRY BIGG BORN 7th MARCH 1809 AT REST 27th JUNE 1888. MAKE THEM TO BE NUMBERED WITH THY SAINTS IN GLORY EVERLASTING". To the immediate right of this tomb is a hewn cross inscribed- "AUGUSTA BIGG BORN 22nd MAY 1889 ENTERED UNTO REST 14th JANUARY 1922". This is daughter Augusta. Next to this is another cross bearing the inscription "HARRIET ANN CURTIS NOVEMBER 17th 1887". And finally, on the far right, is a large canopied crucifix inscribed- "IN LOVING MEMORY FREDERICK BIGG 21st JUNE 1925 AGED 78 REST IN PEACE, JESU MERCY", and at its foot " ALSO OF ROSE BIGG HIS WIFE DIED 28th JULY 1948 AGED 83".

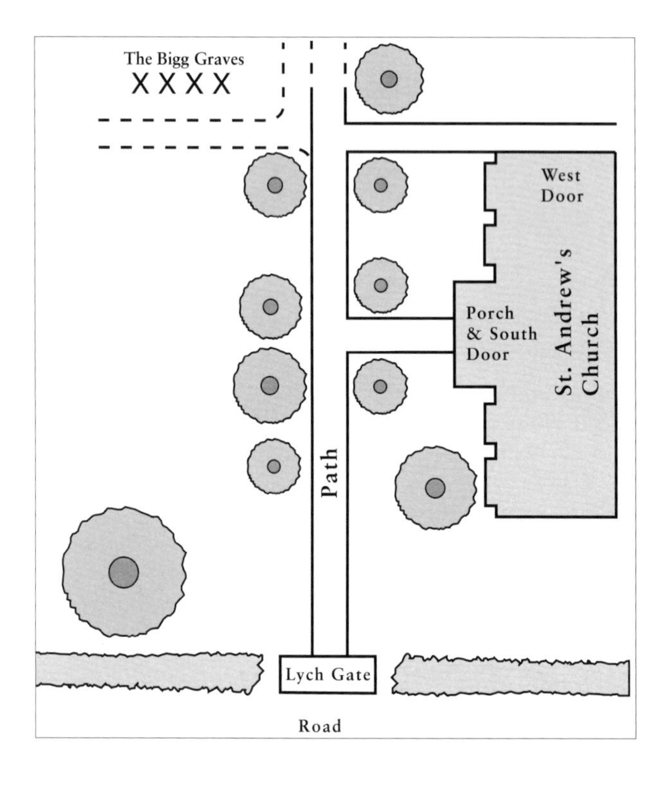

Diagram showing location of the Bigg and Curtis graves in the churchyard at Nuthurst.

The Bigg graves as they were found at St Andrew's in 1999. *Photo - Tony Turner*

The four graves are cleared to reveal inscriptions, in 1999. *Photo - Tony Turner*

Chapter Seven
Frederick's Story

The third son and youngest child of Smith Henry and Augusta was Frederick, who had been born at Swallowfield on the 8th July 1846. Augusta's diary records the event as follows:-

"...at about 7 pm my baby was born and on the whole considering the immense size of the child, I was thankful I did not suffer more than I did. The elder children had gone to relations except poor little Henry very sick, had his throat lanced and above a tablespoon of matter came from it, and he behaved very well and it is to be kept open with linseed poultices three times a day".

The new baby was baptised at St. Andrew's Church, Nuthurst on 28th October that year.

Frederick lived at Swallowfield until the age of 39 when he married Rose, daughter of Frederick Thomas Curtis, Solicitor and his second wife, Mary Sicard nee Delmar. In fact Rose was his second cousin once removed, and was very much younger than her husband; Rose had been born in 1865, and was only 20 when she married Frederick in 1885.

Frederick and Rose had no children. Frederick chose the Army as his career, like his older brother William. He joined the Royal Regiment of Artillery, served much of his Army life at Woolwich Arsenal in Kent and rose to the rank of Major.

As the youngest of a family of five, and the youngest of four sons, Frederick would not normally have contemplated inheriting Swallowfield, but that unlikely event happened just a few short months after his marriage in 1885 when his father, Smith Henry Bigg passed away on 22nd November at the age of 83. It came about because Henry was well settled far away with his own property in Australia, Edward was already well provided for as the owner of The Hyde estate and poor William had died some four years earlier. We must surmise that Smith Henry had judged that Henry and Edward had already been provided for, and had accordingly settled his estate (Swallowfield) on the youngest son.

Taking up the challenge of managing the estate at Swallowfield, Frederick resigned his commission and left the Army with the rank of Major, Retired.

Two years later in 1887, Miss Harriet Ann Curtis, the mutual aunt of both Frederick and Rose, died whilst at Swallowfield in the November, to be followed a year later by Frederick's mother Augusta. Both sisters are buried in the churchyard at St. Andrew's, Nuthurst.

With both their parents gone, the surviving children (Henry, Augusta, Edward and Frederick) dedicated two fine stained glass windows to their memory, which can be found behind the altar in the Church of the Good Shepherd at Mannings Heath i.e the little church Augusta had built in memory of her brother William in 1881.

Frederick and Rose spent the rest of their lives managing Swallowfield. In addition to farming Swallowfield, Frederick also purchased Cook's Farm which is situated opposite the church of St. Andrew in Nuthurst. He was a keen sportsman with interests in shooting and golf. Both Swallowfield and the Cook's estate offered excellent game shooting and many shooting parties were held there over the years. His young nephews in particular were always pleased to visit and enjoyed the woodland and all that Swallowfield had to offer by way of outdoor pursuits.

Frederick was a keen golfer and in 1896 was one of a group who formed the West Park Golf Club at Handcross, a 12 hole course within five miles of Crawley Railway Station, and very close to his brother Edward's home at The Hyde. The golf club at Mannings Heath was already in being and the course was re-opened in the early 1920s; part of it had been ploughed up during World War I.

Frederick and Rose continued to live at Swallowfield as the years turned and the new century arrived, with Major Bigg engaging himself in Parish matters

During these years they entertained a number of visitors from the Antipodes including Frederick's Australian nephew, Henry's son, Alfred Edward Bigg, his wife Mabel and their three oldest children who visited them in 1907.

In the same way that Henry had returned to the family home at Swallowfield in 1876 after 20 years absence, so his son Alfred brought his wife and children to Swallowfield, from Swallowfield NSW, 31 years later. Unfortunately it wasn't simply a case of pilgrimage, but was occasioned by the need for Mabel to seek specialist treatment for a serious back injury.

She had been an expert horsewoman but had been thrown from her horse and crushed when it had reared up unexpectedly and fallen on her. The help she sought was not productive, however, and she was confined to a wheelchair for the last years of her life.

The return trips to Swallowfield by the Australian branch of the family continued. During the First World War, between 1914 and 1918, one of Alfred's children, Edward Lionel Bigg (known as Lionel), now a grown man and serving as a Trooper in the 1st Light Horse Regiment, was able to call in during his leave to pay his respects to Frederick and Rose. Apparently he found Frederick rather intimidating, and Lionel was not easily intimidated! When Lionel married in 1919 Frederick sent a carriage clock as a wedding present. Lionel had hoped for something more substantial. The clock proved to be cantankerous and was promptly called "Uncle Fred" after its giver. It is now in the possession of Keith Bigg, who says it needs a new spring.

Having looked after the estate for some 40 years, Frederick died on 21st June 1925 at the age of 78. He was amongst the first in the area to be cremated. Burial was the norm at this time, but Frederick was cremated at Brookwood, near Woking in Surrey. His ashes were brought back to Nuthurst.

Under the provisions of his will there were many legacies, including some relating to his service life i.e one to a Lt. Vere Welch of the London Rifle Brigade and another to Miss E Newman who was the daughter of the late General W Newman, described as the father of HM Artillery. Miss Newman used to visit Swallowfield once a year The beneficiaries of interest to our story are mentioned on the right. (NB The list is not complete.)

Beneficiary	Relationship	Amount	Comments
Rose Bigg	Wife and Executrix	£5,000 and £2,000 pa and all property.	Occupancy of Swallowfield
Alfred Edward	Nephew	£1,000 and all property after death of Rose (except for Cooks Farm).	If Alfred should predecease Frederick, Alfred's oldest son would inherit.
Children of Alfred Edward Bigg (i.e two daughters and four sons).		2/3rds of residue of estate.	
Children of Augusta Emily (Amy) Curtis (i.e three daughters and two sons).		1/3rd of residue of estate.	
Augusta Emily (Amy) Curtis.	Niece, wife of Henry Curtis.	£100	
Mary MacCarogher	Daughter of former Rector of Nuthurst.	£200	
Mrs Laker	Widow of late Peter Laker, Bailiff.	£15 pa	
J Baldwin	Chauffeur.	£100	
Servants (indoor and outdoor)		1 months wages each.	Provided they were in service at his death and had been in service for more than two years.
Servants (indoor and outdoor)		£2,000	Annuities as decided by Rose in her will.
The Alexandra Children's Hospital.		£1,000	
Brighton County Hospital.		£1,000	
Cancer Hospital.		£1,000	
Dr Barnados Homes		£1,000	
Governesses Benevolent Institute		£1,000	
Horsham Cottage Hospital.		£300 and £1,000	
London Lock Hospital and Rescue Home[18]		£1,000	
Salvation Army.		£1,000	

18. *The legacy to The London Lock Hospital and Rescue Home provides a clue to the likely illness that afflicted his brother William.*

Cooks Farm was to be sold off after Rose's death and the proceeds held in trust together with his other residuary personal estate.[19] Besides the legacies above mentioned £15,000 was to be put in trust to provide income to Winifred Edith Wauton for life. She also received a legacy of £500. (Her brother, Hubert O. Wauton, had been killed when commanding HMS Falcon off the coast of Belgium in 1914. There is a plaque to his memory next to the South door of St. Andrew's church at Nuthurst, that was erected by Major Bigg.)

As regards the £2,000 set aside for the servants, Frederick provided the funds but asked that Rose, in her will, should decide by what amounts each servant should benefit. He wanted the servants who remained on after his death - until his wife's death - to benefit, unless they had been released by Rose on the grounds of age, infirmity or sickness. (Even those who fell into this category were catered for by Frederick.) Frederick anticipated that Rose might default on this "direction" in his will, so he stated that in these circumstances (i.e should Rose fail to decide) his trustees should in their absolute discretion make the decision as to who should benefit and to what extent. At the time of Frederick's death his servants on hearing of their good fortune in sharing the very substantial sum of £2,000 must have thought they had won the lottery. But of course they could not receive any share until Rose had died. Unfortunately for them (but fortunately for Rose) she didn't die for many years, and they had to wait an awfully long time before they benefited from Frederick's generosity.

In fact Rose, Frederick's widow, remained on at Swallowfield for another 23 years after his death, until her demise in 1948, at the age of 83. Their graves adjoin the other Bigg family memorials in the churchyard of St. Andrew's, Nuthurst.

As it transpired, Rose did not fail to conform to Frederick's wishes concerning the servants. She determined that the £2,000 should be apportioned as follows:-

To Jesse Baldwin	£600
To Alfred Dancy	£500
To John Jenner	£400
To Alfred Flint	£300
To Allen Flint	£200

Even 23 years after Frederick had expired the sums were still large. The Chauffeur (Mr Baldwin) bought his house at the corner of Church Road and the A281, and Allen Flint recalls he could have bought a house for £ 200 at the time, but decided against it in the end.

19. *Cooks Farm was sold by Frederick before he died to Col. McKergow, who in turn sold it to Capt. Luke Smith a few years later.*

Besides these amounts Rose gave 22 primary legacies (i.e money) and over 30 specific legacies (i.e identified items). Most of the primary legacies were to members of the Curtis and Delmar families, although her Godson, John Bigg, received £50. Among the lesser amounts were the following:-

Primary legacies

Treasurer of the Nuthurst Parochial Church Council (to be applied in any manner the Council think proper.)	£100
Nuthurst District Nursing Association (for general purposes.)	£35
Society for the Propagation of the Gospel in Foreign Parts (for their Medical Missions.)	£30
Mannings Heath Football Club.	£5
Mannings Heath Cricket Club.	£5
Mannings Heath Womens Institute.	£6

Specific legacies

These included clocks, several items of silverware, a fur coat, an inlaid card table, pictures, carpets, furniture and bed linen. All items of apparel not otherwise disposed of were to go to Miss Smallwood's Society for the Assistance of Ladies in Reduced Circumstances.

Again, the servants were remembered-

- Jesse Baldwin, her Chauffeur, was given her car, twelve gallons of petrol and the furniture in his room over the garage. (The car was a large Fiat, according to Allen Flint.)
- Alice Baldwin, his wife, received a carved oak cupboard, a pair of blankets, an eiderdown quilt and a carpet.
- Their daughters were given a small oak table.
- Alfred and Annie Dancy were given a military chest of drawers and a desk.
- Bertha Riddle, Edith Stoner and Henrietta Howett (her three maids) were invited to take their bed linen off their respective beds and another item of their choice from their bedrooms. They were also given 3 months wages, in addition to any wages owing.
- Bertha and Edith were also given £40 each, and Henrietta £25.
- Each full-time member of staff working outdoors in service at Rose's death received one month's wages, in addition to any owing.

The gross value of her estate was £12,226-17-9d.

Major Frederick Bigg, youngest son of Smith Henry and Augusta Bigg, in uniform.

Rose Curtis as a child.

Rose in later life.

Shooting party outside The Hyde. Major Frederick Bigg is on the left in doorway. *Photo - Pat Curtis*

The marriage of Frederick and Rose, in 1885.

PART TWO

In Part One of the Story of Swallowfield we have followed the fortunes of Smith Henry Bigg, his wife Augusta and their five children.

As we have seen, daughter Augusta remained a spinster, William died a bachelor, and of the three sons who married it was only Henry (by then in Australia) who produced offspring who survived to adulthood. Edward's four children had died at an early age, while Frederick's marriage was not blessed with children.

So now our story has to divide. We are left with two distinct avenues to follow. With the death of Frederick (in 1925) and his wife Rose 23 years later, the descendants of Smith Henry in the UK finish and all we are left with to follow in England are the lovely properties that were once owned by the Bigg family - The Hyde and Swallowfield.

In Part Two of our story we will see what happened to these two fine estates, and also take a passing look at the Church of the Good Shepherd.

Then, in Part Three we will pick up the thread of Henry's descendants in Australia, and learn what happened to the other Swallowfield, the one in New South Wales.

Part Two

Chapter Eight
The Hyde

Swallowfield at Mannings Heath was, of course, the second Sussex country estate of the Bigg family; the first and foremost was The Hyde.

The Bigg family in the Crawley area goes back a long way. In 1332 among the names in a Subsidy Roll of the area was a John Bygge, and in 1373 a Thomas Bygge/Bigg atte Hyde sued a John Mayne for certain lands in Slagham, now Slaugham, (pronounced Slaffham.)

The first firm record we have of The Hyde estate being in the Bigg family goes back to Edward Bigg, born in 1760, whose 12th child was Smith Henry Bigg. In Chapter 1 we saw that this Edward Bigg lived in London with his wife Sarah and their large family. He became a solicitor and started his own practice. He was very successful at his profession and had offices in London, as well as a house at 45 Tavistock Square, London. He also acquired The Hyde, a large country estate in Sussex. Apparently one of his pastimes was to look over houses being demolished in London and to buy up antiques and pieces of furniture that took his fancy, which he then used extensively to refurbish The Hyde. The wonderful staircase is supposed to have found its way to the house in this manner.

When he died in 1823, his estate passed to his eldest surviving son, Edward Smith Bigg, a bachelor (and Smith Henry's brother), then aged only 23.

Edward Smith Bigg, also a solicitor by profession, was in due course just as successful as his father before him, perhaps more so. On inheriting his father's estate he was a wealthy man, but as we will see he had the vision and foresight to see a new business opportunity that could be developed from his existing profession and make him even more prosperous.

A year after taking over his father's practice he moved it from 29 to 38 Southampton Buildings where he carried on the business alone until 1839, when he took a partner. This was a John William Goldfinger, who had for the previous two years been in practice there on his own and also at 8 Bartholomew Place, Kentish Town. (Goldfinger, however, may have died in 1841 for after that date his name no longer appears in the Law Lists, or any other public record.)

Edward's practice was an extensive one and, as might be expected from the inheritor of a business whose clients affairs had for over a century been conducted by members of the Bigg family, it was mostly concerned with conveyancing, trusts, wills, insurance etc. Bigg's personal standing among members of the profession was high and his knowledge of financial affairs generally was widely respected. By 1845 he found it necessary to recruit partners to share the increasing workload. Accordingly, in that year he took as partners two young men who had been admitted as solicitors in 1841. They were Edward Boyle Church and William Atkinson Langdale.

The new business opportunity that Edward conceived concerned fire insurance. In the early 19th century there was a growing need for fire insurance cover for buildings of all types (but principally residential and commercial properties) and their contents. The demand for this facility was particularly well appreciated by lawyers. In considering the matter they were aware that by their function they could occupy a particularly important strategic position in any such situations. First of all, their members were already in professional contact with the great mass of probable subscribers. Secondly, members of their profession could probably be readily induced to act as agents. Thirdly, with their local knowledge, bad risks could be identified and rejected, whilst excessive claims for compensation could be monitored and, if necessary, litigated and controlled. There were, of course, already in existence several fire insurance societies when, in 1845, discussion on the proposal reached finality and The Law Fire Insurance Society was formally established. All things considered, it seemed certain that, if properly administered (and having regard to the fact that costs of administration were likely to be lower than those of many of their competitors already in the field), it should become a strong competitor. And it did. In due course over the next century and a half it expanded and developed rapidly to become eventually one of the world's leading insurance companies, the powerful Royal & SunAlliance.

The archives of The Law Fire Insurance Society (held in the Guildhall Manuscript Library) are, fortunately, well preserved and complete. The Deed of Settlement (MS15002) dated 22nd November 1845 provided for 20 directors of whom 16 were solicitors and 4 were barristers. The Chairman was Sir George Rose who was a judge in the court of bankruptcy and Master in Chancery. The Society's capitalisation composed 50,000 shares of £100 each, the maximum holding being 100 shares. They were all taken up by members of the profession. Edward Smith Bigg was appointed a director, holding the maximum permissible number of shares.

The preponderance of shareholders were in London. Among the country members was Leonard Edward Bigg of the Bristol firm of Bigg, Meade and Co. who had 50 shares. Three solicitors and one barrister named Tatham - all with addresses in Highgate - were subscribers and one of them, Meaburn Tatham of the firm Tatham, Upton & Johnston of Great Winchester Street and 24 Lincolns Inn, was appointed a director.

The Board met weekly and the Minutes show that the Society's affairs were subjected to close scrutiny and tight control. Not only did Edward Smith Bigg unfailingly attend meetings, but the minutes also show him to have been a leading Board member. His opinion was sought on such matters as to whether the solicitor's bill of costs for work in forming the Society was reasonable (after scrutiny by Edward it was reduced by £470), but also as to the soundness of certain prospective insurance propositions. And when, in 1847, the Society decided to seek new premises, the Board appointed Bigg *"to consider proposals for acquiring a site in Chancery Lane from the Incorporated Law Society"*.

A list of applicants for fire insurance and the amount of cover sought was placed before the Board at each weekly meeting. At the first such meeting the proposals considered were from, inter alia, Lord Harris (£11,500), Lord Saye and Sele (£12,000), Earl Lonsdale (£15,500), General Sir George Otway (£16,000), Viscount Ponsonby

(£8,500) and W. Wilson of Grosvenor Square (£32,000). In its first year it had issued cover for risks of almost £7 million, a quite staggering sum. The number of agents (solicitors) appointed in that year was 368. The enterprise had been successfully launched and it continued to grow.

By 1865 the cover provided by the Society was almost £32 million, an enormous sum in today's terms. In the early years the Society's clients were principally members of the aristocratic land-owning fraternity, but as time went on more and more cover was sought by ordinary householders and by members of the business community in respect of offices, shops and factories. The importance of identifying bad risks and false and exaggerated claims then became increasingly important, and it was in that connection that the Society's local agents (i.e members of the legal profession) were often able to provide the Board with valuable local knowledge. Law suits were not uncommon. The Society adopted an increasingly stringent requirement for the inspection of properties before insurance cover was given. There are, in the Minutes, records of such inspections having been made by Edward Smith Bigg personally, when he would comment not only on the character of particular buildings and their owners, but also on those adjacent properties and their occupants. Fires do not recognise curtilages! Enlightened self interest, of course, also merited close co-operation with those bodies which were being established to provide for fire fighting forces, and the adoption of exacting safety standards in building construction, etc.

Edward's preoccupation with the Society's affairs necessarily took up an increasingly large proportion of his time, though fees paid to directors were only nominal. His law firm - now styled as Bigg, Church and Langdale - was concurrently benefiting from the surging economic activity of the period. Being a bachelor and already wealthy he decided to leave the partnership in 1847, and to move from London for the less hectic environment of Crawley. Thus, his journeys to attend the Law Fire Insurance Society's weekly meetings in the City enabled him from his retirement at the age of 46, until his death at 71, still to keep in touch with the world of affairs in which he was always so fully involved.

The name Bigg then was extinguished from the partnership name. But not permanently; for another holder of the name was to appear in it again from 1862 to 1882.

This lengthy explanation shows how the two brothers, Edward Smith Bigg and Smith Henry Bigg, both occupying country estates in Sussex, were really in different leagues when it came to business, wealth and good fortune. Edward had inherited his wealth, but he was a very astute and competent businessman, as well as a highly regarded lawyer. Being a bachelor meant that his finances were not drawn upon by the natural demands occasioned by supporting a wife and raising a family. However, he did support his unmarried sisters for most of their lives and provide them with a home at The Hyde in their later years. Edward's wealth compounded through his interest in the Law Fire Insurance Society, in which as we have seen he was a founder member and a leading director.

On the other hand, Smith Henry Bigg tried to emulate his brother's life-style, with neither the wealth to support his ambition, nor the good fortune that is needed sometimes to avoid life's pitfalls. Virtually nothing seemed to go right for Smith Henry and his children until they reached later life, when inheritances came to their rescue.

The census for the Slaugham District in 1851 shows The Hyde being occupied by-

- Edward Smith Bigg JP unmarried aged 51
- Sarah A. Bigg, sister, unmarried, aged 60
- Ellen E. Bigg, sister, unmarried, aged 54
- Lucy M Bigg, sister, unmarried, aged 53
- as well as 6 servants.

The Court Roll of the Manor of Slaugham shows that in 1851 he purchased two houses and 17 acres to add to his estate there.

Ellen and Sarah, two of Edward's sisters, died in 1865 at The Hyde, and they were followed in February 1871 by Edward himself, aged 71.[19] It was their sister Lucy Maria who lived on there until her death in May 1875, when at the age of 77 she drowned in a lake on the estate.

As we have seen in Chapter 5 (Edward's Story), it was Smith Henry's second son, Edward, who inherited The Hyde estate and moved there in 1875. Four children were born to Edward and his wife, but none survived. When Edward died in 1907, the property passed to his widow Fanny, but when she died in 1922, The Hyde passed out of the Bigg family for ever.[20]

The Hyde was originally within the ancient St. Leonard's forest. It is mentioned as a Shooting Lodge in 1760. It still stands in just under 1,000 acres. It is a large country house, with about 16 bedrooms, surrounded by a large garden and many outbuildings, stables, fields etc., The gardens were always beautifully laid out and maintained, although now they are past their glory. Inside the house are extensive woodcarvings and panelling, particularly around the stairs and in the library. The Hyde estate is just off the A23, the main London to Brighton road (see map at Foreword.)

The Hyde estate is half woodland and half arable land, with forest soils. The fields are not concentrated, but scattered among the woodland areas.

In 1842 The Hyde was enlarged by the architect Sir William Tite, who at that time was renovating the Temple Church (of Norman origin) in London. It was as a consequence of this that some very old, damaged Purbeck marble pillars from the church found their way to The Hyde and were incorporated into the hall and stair area in a way that conceals their defacement. The porch also has a number of delightful angel heads carved in the stone inside, at the top.

19. Incidentally, Edward's death gave rise to a problem for his descendants. Edward's father, Edward Bigg, had in his will appointed his son (Edward Smith Bigg) and his two eldest daughters to be his executors with directions "to sell the houses in Fenchurch Buildings and convert same into cash to be considered part of my estate". However, Edward died in 1871 without complying with his father's directions. This resulted in litigation, which was reported in the London Gazette of 21st May 1872.

20. Edward's estate at his death included some 20 houses in addition to The Hyde.

When Smith Henry's house, Swallowfield, a few miles down the road from The Hyde was finished in 1845 it was strikingly similar in appearance to The Hyde - which would lead us to think that Sir William Tite also had a hand in the building alterations to Swallowfield. It is unusual for windows in houses of the period to take the form of church windows, featuring an arched top and single mullion. Yet The Hyde and Swallowfield both have church-type windows. This could be co-incidence, but knowing that Sir William Tite was related to the Bigg family, designed churches, and had re-designed The Hyde makes it highly likely that he influenced on the re-building work at Swallowfield commissioned by Smith Henry, but this has not been established for certain.

The Hyde was purchased in 1922 by Colonel J.R.Warren and his wife. Col. Warren had been brought up at the nearby larger property of Handcross Park, which was owned by his bachelor uncle, John Warren. (Col. Warren had gone to live there as a small boy with his mother and father at the invitation of John Warren.) He qualified as a barrister, played sport well (particularly cricket) and served in the Army, being wounded in the First World War. He bought The Hyde estate after the war with the intention of farming it, but the house was not needed and initially he let it. He was a very successful farmer and came to breed a prize-winning herd of Sussex cattle. Bulls from this herd were exported far afield, including to South Africa and Canada. He became well known as a forward-thinking agriculturist and the workers' cottages he had built won prizes for their modern, yet attractive design. After owning The Hyde for two years Col. Warren fell in love and married, and decided to move into the house, resulting in the tenants having to be displaced. The Colonel and his wife, Eveline, had two children, Michael and Mary, both of whom were born in the older part of the house.

Between the two wars, Col. Warren quietly and conscientiously pursued a personal mission to assist those of his Regiment (The Royal Sussex Regiment) who fell on hard times, and sorely needed help. In the years following the end of the First World War, the employment situation in the United Kingdom was desperate, as tens of thousands of soldiers returned from the trenches at the same time as the war economy was reverting to peacetime levels, with dramatic consequences. Those who had been injured, in body or mind, fared particularly badly, as there was a surplus of able-bodied men stepping forward for each vacancy

Wherever possible he helped them, taking them on at the estate if he could, so that there always seemed to be one or two men around The Hyde who were amputees, or were crippled, on crutches, or who had been gassed.

When the Second World War broke out in 1939 the family knew that the Government would be likely to requisition Handcross Park, or The Hyde, or perhaps even both. Daily in the early months of the Phoney War they waited in trepidation for the brown official envelope to drop on the mat, or for the telephone call, which would tell them what was to happen. In the event it came as a ring of the bell of The Hyde one winter's evening when the two children were playing trains in the large hall. The caller was a Major who, after the briefest of introductions, very quickly dropped to his knees and became engrossed with the children and their train set! Eventually it was Colonel Warren who broke the spell, suggesting that the Major and he should probably best retire to the study room to discuss business. The Colonel was keen to surrender The Hyde, rather than to give up Handcross Park, because his aged mother was still living there and, understandably, he did not want her disturbed. But this did not suit the Army. It was pointed out to him that The Hyde was smaller, and with its two steep hills and narrow road entrances, would not be as suitable for tanks. So it transpired that The Hyde was saved from being requisitioned. Col. Warren and his wife brought his mother and some of her staff over from Handcross Park, to join his family and staff for the duration, and the Army took over Handcross Park.

In addition to the folk coming over from Handcross Park, there were others who came to fill the house and create an unusual mixture of souls. A number of relatives moved down from London to The Hyde, and six evacuees and their teacher were billeted there as well, when their school was temporarily relocated to the Handcross area.

Because of his war wounds the Colonel was not called up, but nevertheless, like everyone else, did what he could towards furthering the war effort. He stayed in close touch with the various Officers who were responsible for Handcross Park, and this personal relationship helped prevent that property from being too badly damaged during its occupancy by the Army. (After the war, the Colonel took some delight in recounting that it was not the Canadians stationed there that caused the problems, but the ATS girls!)

Col. Warren became Chairman of East Sussex Council among other appointments, and Mrs Warren was Deputy Controller of the Women's Voluntary Service for Sussex.

The Hyde was not a target for enemy bombers but it did have its share of close shaves. There were military targets not far away, and being en route to London, there were several occasions when jettisoned bomb loads were scattered in the area by enemy aircraft turning back and aborting their missions. The closest call came one night when a loud crack was heard outside causing everyone to rush outside to "action stations". The noise was caused by a stick of incendiary bombs that had fallen across the tennis court, only missing the house by a few yards. The great fear was that incendiaries would be dropped on the roof, and become lodged in the many gables where they would have been inaccessible to those trying to extinguish the fires that would have been started.

Although it was not requisitioned by the Army, The Hyde served as a refuge for evacuees from the air raids. As the plaque in All Saints Church, Handcross, records, children and staff from Buckingham Gate School in London were very grateful for the facilities in the Parish when they were evacuated there to get away from the blitz. A great number of local houses and cottages in Slaugham Parish were given Buckingham Gate children to look after, and if a family could manage a certain number, they had a teacher too.

The Colonel's ambition to extend The Hyde, which he had intended to do in the late 1930s, was left unfulfilled, mainly because of the war. He had copious quantities of Horsham stone at his disposal and had his heart set on making the house even larger. It was, of course, already a large property and took several staff to service it and to attend to the guests who were always staying for one reason or another. It seemed a continuous round of House, Dinner and Shooting parties. Before the war the permanent staff included a head cook (or chef), a kitchen maid, a scullery maid, a butler, a head house maid and three assistants, an odd-job man who stoked the two boilers, cleaned shoes and helped around the house in numerous ways - as well as a large team of estate workers.

Michael and Mary Warren, the Colonel and Mrs Warren's two children, grew up on the estate and look back on it as a magical and beautiful place. Michael eventually took a farm of his own near Barcombe in Sussex when he married.

Col. Warren died at the age of 68 in 1956, succumbing to his war wounds and to a heart condition. In 1961 a gift to the Parish church was given in his memory.

Mrs Eveline Warren remained at The Hyde and, before she married, her daughter Mary and her friends were often there too at weekends and holidays. In Mrs Warren's lifetime the extensive and beautiful gardens were regularly opened to the public in aid of the District Nurse Scheme. Handcross Park was sold in 1957.

In the same way that her husband gave comfort to men of his regiment, Mrs Warren made The Hyde available to a variety of friends and relations who needed to convalesce, or simply wanted to come to stay there with their children. The delights of such a wonderful house, gardens and estate were still attractive and captivated all who visited. With ponies to ride and boats to take on the lake it was a wonderland for young people and adults alike and the house gardens and woods would ring with the laughter and chatter of youngsters enjoying riotous games.

Before finishing this chapter on The Hyde it is worth reflecting on those lost days of yore, when the house and estate was in its heyday, when children were perhaps playing their version of "Swallows and Amazons". One piece of correspondence can help us see back to those times, around the turn of the century (circa 1900), through the eyes of someone who was there. Here is a letter written by a Miss Helen Conway who stayed at The Hyde at various times in the first 18 years of her life, when Fanny and Edward Francis Bigg were still there. In July 1962 she went back to visit The Hyde and was met by Eveline Warren. Her letter of thanks, and its attachment, creates a perfect cameo, a charming picture in miniature of a Sussex country house in Victorian times seen through the eyes of a child.

3 Curling Vale,
Onslow Village,
10th July 1962 *Guildford.*

Dear Mrs Warren,

I do want to thank you so very much for your kindness in allowing my nephew and me to see the gardens of The Hyde yesterday morning before they were really open to the public. We saw the "Garden Open" notice at the entrance to the back drive as we were on our way to lunch with cousins at Hayward Heath.

I have always longed to be able to see The Hyde again, and to visit it yesterday was the greatest treat. How truly lovely you have made it! Of course, I hardly recognised it at all - except the well-remembered kitchen gardens. I only wish we had had more time. We had planned to come back again after tea - but unhappily had a puncture in Handcross and were stuck there for over an hour! We were most disappointed - but had to give up the idea.

I first stayed at The Hyde first when I was 2 months old, and every year after that until I was 18. Mrs Bigg ("Aunt Fanny" to us) was a first cousin of my grandmother. My parents always loved the Hyde and we children of course had a wonderful time in the fields and woods, and paddling about the lake in a very derelict punt. Our cousins used to stay there at the same time, and we all ran wild out of doors, but had to behave very correctly in the house! I expect all our friends on the staff - Weller, Webb, Langridge, Ashby, and Mary Ann and Libby - must have died long ago.

I wonder who laid out your beautiful grounds. He certainly was a genius.

Please forgive me for writing this. I just feel I must say "thank you". Of course this needs no reply.

Yours sincerely,

(Miss) Helen Conway

THE ATTACHMENT - An essay written by Helen Conway to Mr Murray Marsden concerning The Hyde.

"...Your letter has charmed me back into days which were so good. Days when we went with our parents and Nanny (little pious Nanny, who hung texts above our beds- who was never "angry" with us, but only "grieved",- which was so much more distressing - and who scared me, as a very small girl, by telling me of The Guardian Angel at the foot of my bed: (later on I got to like him) - well, we all went by train, complete with a huge number of those black round-topped trunks, and a bath which I think was called a "hip-bath" ; anyway, it was hinged and went up at the back rather like an arm-chair with no legs, and was packed full for the journey. Molly and I wore little bonnets in the train, to keep our hair clean: Nanny was very fussy about that. Then when we arrived at Three Bridges we were met by the wagonette, with old Weller on the box, in his dark blue livery with silver buttons, and his top hat with the cockade at the side: I always sat beside him, as horsey smells in carriages and buses of those days always made me in danger of being sick. It was so exciting on the box with Weller that I never thought of being sick. We ambled along for ages, and then turned in to a rhododendron-lined drive, three miles of it, so we were told by our cousins, but surely wasn't true ! but it was a very long drive. And at the end of it people in the porch to welcome us, - and some moments of panic-shyness for me, always a timid child - and then the parents left us and we three and Nanny went through the green baize door and up the back-stairs to the Nursery: where we were washed and taken by Nanny to the Kitchen or to the rather terrifying "Servants Hall", to say "How do you do " to the cook of the day, and to our beloved friends, Mary Ann and her sister Libby (with the intriguing club foot) and to Webb the butler. Then to the housekeeper's room, and a riot of cousins, some older, some younger, weren't good like us; they rubbed their bread and butter in the remains of their jam, and Nanny was constantly "grieved" ! We three always deteriorated during the three weeks. Out of doors next day we rushed down to the "Boat House Lake" (one of the three Hammer Ponds - the other two being the "Water Lily Lakes") and out on the lake in the rather derelict punt, in the charge of our elder cousins: and there were the acres of woods, and the rusty streams where if you poked with a stick bubbles came up, smelling somewhat metallic, and we were told it was iron in the soil; and Ashby the game-keeper to visit in his cottage deep in the woods, with his billy-cock hat, his beard and gaiters and gun. And there was the little iron gate which led to the three huge kitchen gardens, edged with hot-smelling box, where Langridge, bearded and of necessity rather fierce, reigned, and carried on perpetual war with our red-headed cousin Meg, who stole his gooseberries; and the greenhouses, one with a vine and one with nectarines, locked against us unless escorted by a grown-up. And there was the Nut Walk, and the huge Wellingtonia (I think) tree with the wooden seat encircling it, where we all sat, and where Webb the butler, who spoiled us, brought us plates of cake and fruit: and the day when in the middle of the feast the dragon of the establishment, the grim Aunt Maude, was seen approaching and everything had to be hidden under the seat behind all our legs. Meg and her brother Rob climbed that immense Wellingtonia and stuck a pin in the top to show they'd reached it. There was the "dressing-bell" which so often found us far away, and the scrimmage to get back in time for the wonderful but formal - and silent, for our part -

meals which we had in the big dining-room with the grown-ups: burly Uncle Edward at the head of the table, with his little terrier who always sat behind him on his chair: Uncle Edward whom I loved and was not shy of because he spoke so little, and who once greeted my parents with " Well, my dears, I thought we'd be seeing you here today; your Auntie's been putting your photographs out." And the delicate, pretty Aunt Fannie at the other end of the table, my grandmother's cousin, with a somewhat severe manner, but with a twinkling eye.

Before breakfast there were "Prayers", read by Uncle Edward, and the procession of servants led by Cook and ending with Webb and his page-boy; and the moment when at half-time we all turned round to kneel, the servants in their full, starched frocks, mauve-and-white striped, and stiff high caps, and Libby having trouble with her club-foot. Usually about twenty visitors were there: our day "Dad" the ring-leader of the men. And always the three sweet Eyre sisters - Ruth, Margery and Phyllis (who is now wife of that Clarence Elliott whose "courageous" face you liked in the "Countryman") who used to lean out of the window of the Oak Room in the darkening summer evenings and sing trios in their lovely fresh voices, with the rest of the party (and we were allowed there too) sitting below on the terrace, with the smell of the geraniums in their tubs - a smell which never fails to take me back there. Three large flies there were in the ointment of those visits:- the day — unknown to us - on which Aunt Fanny would appear in the Nursery and require the two of us to "repeat our Catechism"; the evening on which we were taken dressed in our best to the drawing-room, there to play our "Piece" on the piano; and the early hours of the night spent miserably in the huge oak four-poster in the Oak Room, with its carved cherubs and scrolls, waiting for my Mother to come up, she being so nervous to sleep alone. It goes without saying that I never told anyone about the ghosts I saw and the creakings I heard, or I should have been promptly put back in the Nursery with Molly.

Well - so much for memories. It's your fault for evoking them."

When Mrs Eveline Warren died in 1977 the difficult decision as to what to do with The Hyde had to be faced. No one wanted to sell it, and all the family regarded it as a treasure, but on the other hand it was a huge house and far too big for the normal domestic needs of any one of them. So, for a year it was only occupied occasionally by friends using it for a holiday now and then.

The question of what to do with it was solved around the time of the Lambeth Conference of 1978. The Warren family were, and are, committed Christians and Christian families are known to have lived in the house since 1842. There had been a definite continuation of worship, witness and outreach at The Hyde since that time. (In their lifetime Edward and Fanny had a lot to do with the buildings and upkeep of nearby All Saints Church in Handcross, as the two wall plaques in the church confirm, and likewise windows and plaques in Slaugham Church testify to their involvement with that church.) It transpired that in 1977 the Warren family came into contact with Colin Urquhart, an Anglican vicar, and his community of followers who were living together as a Christian group in Luton. He and his Bethany Fellowship urgently needed to find a new home, where they could continue to live out their lives as a community. The Hyde was perfect, offering spacious living accommodation, a peaceful and tranquil setting, and facilities for communal functions and training. With great speed arrangements were made for the Bethany Fellowship to lease the buildings, and they moved in. The arrangement proved to be very successful and the Fellowship (later to change its name to the Kingdom Faith) expanded rapidly.

By the time 1986 came, they had outgrown even The Hyde, and left to move into the RSPCA College a few miles away, in Roffey.

After the Bethany Fellowship left an Open Afternoon was held at The Hyde so that anyone and everyone who had worked at The Hyde over the years could come back, with their relations, to see the place. It was a great day, with the old house as it had been complete with furnishings, fittings and ornaments. The staff could show their guests round to see what they had done in their various roles, what they had cleaned and polished, where they had slept, what was kept where, and the like.

The estate was particularly hard hit by the great storm which struck south east England on the night of 16th October 1987. In fact, it devastated the woods to such an extent that fallen beeches, chestnuts and oaks (some several hundreds of years old) and shrubs like huge rhododendrons were still being cut, cleared and driven away for 18 months afterwards. The storm also hit the wildlife badly, and many fallow and roe deer were killed by falling trees during that violent and frightening night.

It is believed the woodlands were particularly badly hit because that area of the estate is on high ground. The bits of the forest that were in depressions, and the young plantations, were spared for a short while, but as soon as the force of the wind knocked down the perimeter trees, the wind penetrated inside the stands and swept away huge swathes of trees.

A replanting programme was started soon afterwards, but the extent of the damage to the estate can clearly still be seen today over 12 years later, and it will take decades for the older trees that were lost to be replaced. The wonderful gardens and the shrubbery walks were severely damaged.

The late Colonel Warren's daughter, Mary Habershon, had left The Hyde in 1977, the year she married her husband Kenneth. They stayed in Reigate in Surrey until 1984, and then moved back to The Hyde estate - not to live at the main house - but to live on the estate in a house built by her father in 1930. After the Bethany Fellowship left, The Hyde itself was used by various groups from time to time for Christian gatherings and seminars. In addition, the house has been used by a prayer group from the Parish Church at Slaugham, which met monthly for a number of years.

But still the problem was its size; it was simply too large for a small family. Again the big debate in the family was what to do with it.

Inevitably, though with great reluctance and not a little heartache, the decision was reached in 1996 to sell the buildings immediately around the house - the garage, the barns and outbuildings and the surrounding garden - to developers, but not the estate land or the other farm buildings elsewhere in the estate grounds.

The sale has gone through and the developers have parcelled up various buildings and parts of buildings for resale, while the family continue to retain and manage the estate lands, consisting of woods, lakes and fields. The Hyde itself has been divided into two. The original 1740 area is now one property and the Sir William Tite/Edward Bigg area is the other.

The estate lands continue to be owned by a trust, with various Warren family members and others as Trustees. Grazing rights are let to various sheep farmers, and there is a horse project in one area.

The Warren family still run the estate. Mary Habershon and her husband live in their house on it, and her niece and her husband (Davina and Revd. Peter Irwin-Clark) and family own the rebuilt Ashby's cottage, deep in the woods and mentioned in Helen Conway's essay. So the next two generations of the Warren family are growing up to know and love The Hyde's woods and lakes, and their friends and relations are enjoying riding and using the boats on the lakes in their turn.

The woodlands are actively and progressively managed, and a large replanting programme took place for several years after the great storm referred to earlier. Some areas are left as ancient woodland, some have young mixed hardwoods in tubes for deer protection, and some are fenced mixed-conifer plantations. Many of the estate cottages have been improved and are now let. The estate staff maintain the fences and all the woods, drives and lakesides.

On several occasions when the Warrens still lived at The Hyde they very much enjoyed meeting members of the Bigg family resident in Australia, who would include a visit to The Hyde in their travels to see the wonderful house and estate that featured so prominently in their family history in former generations.

Footnotes:

1. *Mary and Michael Warren donated a new organ to St Mary's, Slaugham in 1979, in affectionate memory of Eveline Warren. Although the instrument was new, part of the Victorian case and pipework was retained. It was dedicated by the Right Reverend The Bishop of Lewes.*

2. *Eveline Warren was born at Chartwell Manor, Westerham, Kent, the home of her uncle, Major Campbell Colquhoun whose family had owned and lived in it since 1848. In 1922 Major Colquhoun sold Chartwell Manor to Winston Churchill, who lived there until his death. In 1947 the house was bought by his friends for his lifetime and later presented to the National Trust.*

3. *At Handcross a Mission Room was dedicated for divine service early in 1876. Prior to this services had been held in a room at "The Red Lion", whilst Sunday School was taken in the old shop opposite. A sanctuary was added to the Mission Room in 1907 by Fanny Bigg, following the death of her husband Edward Francis Bigg earlier that year. The sanctuary was curtained off to allow for secular activities in the other part of the room. In 1914 work began on a Parish Hall, and when this was finished, the Mission Room was transformed into a beautiful little church, chiefly at the kindness of Fanny. The consecration as All Saints took place on 1st November 1915. The east window (by Powell and Co.) was dedicated on 27th November 1922 to the memory of Fanny Bigg, who died on 13th March that year. The memorial window was given by her blood relatives, the Etherington family.*

The South Wing of The Hyde, date unknown.

The lily pool at The Hyde. *Photo - Mary Habershon*

Col. and Eveline Warren and their children, Michael and Mary with Buster above the lily pool at The Hyde in 1937. *Photo - Mary Habershon*

The East Wing of The Hyde in1999. *Photo - Tony Turner*

Spring at The Hyde, 1999. *Photo - Tony Turner*

Chapter Nine
Swallowfield

The house that Smith Henry and Augusta Bigg had built in 1845 at Swallowfield replaced an earlier one; there had been a house called Swallowfield on the same piece of land since 1574, although whether this was the one replaced in 1845 is uncertain. The large uninclosed heathland on the north-eastern corner of the Parish of Nuthurst adjacent to the northern boundary of the Swallowfield estate had gradually been reduced over the 18th century and had been largely reclaimed before 1795. According to local historical records the part of the heathland around Mannings came to be known as Mannings Heath by 1724, and by Smith Henry's day had been reduced to 26 acres of waste land along the two roads that form the crossroads at the centre of today's village of Mannings Heath. In 1841 there were just 30 to 40 houses in Mannings Heath, loosely scattered round the edges of the common, most being in the roads now known as Pound Lane and Golding Lane. Cricket was played in the village by 1840, although the 3 acres for recreation awarded to the Parish did not occur until 1870-1.

The western boundary of the original Bigg estate known as Swallowfield in one direction ran south down the Horsham to Cowfold road (now the A281) to just past the junction with Nuthurst Lane. To the north east it extended along Church Road (as it is now called, following the erection of the Mission Church) as far as the crossroads in Mannings Heath, then east up Winterpit Lane to Seaman's Farm. It included the area now occupied by the pleasant little housing development called the Quarries, which even through to the early part of the 20th century was just that - a stone quarry. Sandstone from the quarry there was used extensively in the area to build homes and other buildings, the most notable of which was St. Hugh's Monastery at Cowfold. Horsham's stone beds were quarried commercially for several centuries for paving and roofing.

When Smith Henry's wife Augusta died in 1888 the Swallowfield estate passed to Frederick, as we have heard in Chapter 7, and Frederick and Rose moved in to join the Augusta the daughter. Some small parcels of the estate were disposed of in due course, Whistley House on the corner of Golding Lane and Winterpit Lane was sold off, as were other areas. A further development of note occurred when Augusta moved away to a house of her own in Mannings Heath, only a 1/4 mile from Swallowfield, immediately to the north of it, called Ryecroft.[21] It was there she died in 1922.

Swallowfield (the house and estate) was sold in 1949, following the death of Rose Bigg, and was purchased by the Goodhews, a well known local family. This broke the Bigg family's ownership of Swallowfield that had lasted uninterrupted for just over a hundred years.

21. *The house known as Ryecroft and its adjoining land was sold off for development in 1983/4 and is now the Whytings, a pleasant estate of 34 houses.*

NORTHLAND FARM
Smithy
DUN HORSE (P.H.)
PO
MANNING'S HEATH
RYECROFT
WOOLMER'S
Copse Cottage
Pt.104 ·194
Pt.104 ·194
WINTERPINK COTTAGE
113 ·837
WINTERPIT
LANE
WALDER'S WOOD
112 3.367
LIMEKILN COPSE
114 5.367
115 3.049
Pt.144
Pt.144 ·131
Pt.143 1.062
146 4.608
161A ·729
160 ·837
158
158 10.833
SWALLOWFIELD
161 13.174
181 1.062
181A 1.672
185
157 5.545
PRESBYTERY
186 ·287
184 ·175

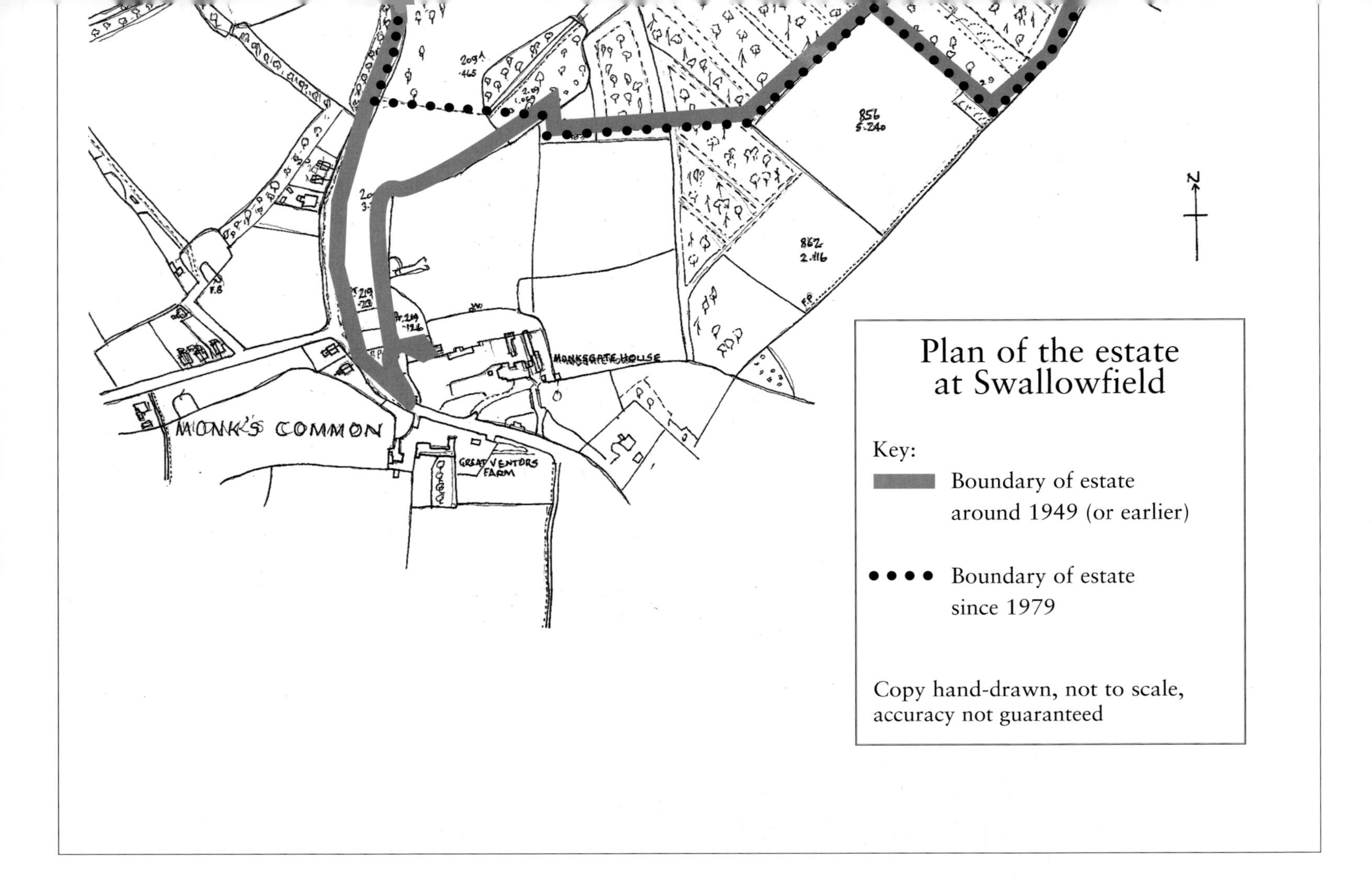
Plan of the estate
at Swallowfield
Key:
Boundary of estate
around 1949 (or earlier)
Boundary of estate
since 1979
Copy hand-drawn, not to scale,
accuracy not guaranteed
N
MONKSGATE HOUSE
MONK'S COMMON
GREAT VENTORS FARM
856
5.240
862
2.116
209A
.465
F.P.
F.B.

But before we finally pass on to successive owners, we should perhaps pause to reflect on life at Swallowfield at the turn of the century. Fortunately we can do better than simply muse at what life was like at Swallowfield in the early 1900s. There are still folk in Mannings Heath today who were part of those times. One such individual is Allen Flint. He still lives in Mannings Heath, only a hundred yards from the rear entrance to the estate.

Allen's parents both worked at Swallowfield and were married in Horsham on 7th January 1908. His father was a Cowman on the estate and his mother a Kitchen Maid. Allen was born on 15th December 1911 and went to work at Swallowfield himself directly after he left school, in November 1926. His first job was as the House and Garden Boy, earning a salary of 15/- per week (75p in today's money.) After two or three years of this work he went on to work in the woods and the estate, where he spent the best part of the next 10 years until enlisting in the Army in 1940, at the time of the Second World War.

Allen has written and published his own memoires about these early days in a booklet called "A Country Village and its People", first published in 1981. He recalls there were six men engaged on outside duties (including himself), a Chauffeur and four Maids making a staff of eleven. In 1940 the staff wages were £120. The Chauffeur and Head Gardener were paid £3 per week each.

The two houses at the end of the drive leading from the north west-side of the estate out on to Church Road (in Mannings Heath) were both owned by the Bigg family, and the one on the junction with the main Horsham - Cowfold road was occupied by the Chauffeur as part of his remuneration.

That particular junction was known as Beggars Bush, and Allen seems to think that it got its name from the hawthorn and ivy thicket that sometimes gave shelter to tramps who used it as they journeyed between the workhouses at Roffey and Cowfold.

Allen's involvement with the woods and estate lands over several years is helpful, since he can recall the creation of the pinetum which was planted with all types of conifers and pines. He was involved in the digging of two ponds, a small round one by the pinetum and a second, deeper one further away which was connected to a number of small canals. Augusta was instrumental in redesigning the woodland areas surrounding the house and the setting out of walks, lily beds, rhododendrons and azalea plots.

Besides a small herd of cattle, the estate was home for numerous wild animals including deer, rabbits, squirrels, badgers and foxes, together with stoats, weasels, mice, moles and voles!

The two sizeable lakes that exist today were not there in the early 1900s. They were low-lying wet areas just inside the perimeter of the woods. It is only in fairly recent times that they have been made into lakes, but the size of the carp (and possibly tench) now in them would suggest the lakes have been around for longer - unless of course they were stocked at some time. The lakes are set in woodland right up to their banks, and with few, if any, visitors to disturb their tranquillity, they are free of paths and the clutter of humans.

In the quiet of an autumnal morning, as the cold white mist clings low to the surface of the lakes like an ethereal quilt, one can easily be transported to the days of Arthurian legend and expect an arm to rise out of the cold waters clutching Excalibur.

Leaving reflections of times long past and returning to the sale of Swallowfield, the new owner, Victor Goodhew also owned property in London, believed to be some hotels; and, as Allen Flint recalls, produce from the large, walled market garden at Swallowfield would be taken up to London once or twice a week for the catering side of the hotel business.

Victor Goodhew became the Member of Parliment for St. Albans in 1959 and went on to hold many ministerial posts and senior appointments. His distinguished career was marked by a Knighthood in 1982.

The Goodhews ran Swallowfield for 30 years, eventually selling it to the Coletta family in 1979.

The Coletta family, John Coletta, his second wife Cherie and their daughter Camilla aged 11 were living in Belgravia in London but looking for a country property, preferably somewhere between London and Brighton. It was Cherie who "found" Swallowfield one day whilst searching for a suitable home and instantly it was accepted as being the right choice for them. John loved it and Camilla adored it. After the usual round of negotiation and legal procedure they moved in to their new home in 1979.

The family loved the house and its estate; Cherie set about re-styling the furnishings, John turned his attention to the estate and Camilla was given what she had for so long yearned for, a horse. And so a palomino pony by the name of Mountain Gold joined the family, as well as a large Old English Sheepdog called Thunder and a cat, Charlie.

In the year that followed Cherie completed her work in the house and John set in place plans to create two new lakes in the lower ground. He was also interested in shooting, which he did as often as he could, given his very hectic and demanding work commitments. John Coletta was in the music business in a big way, managing the very successful Deep Purple rock band, and subsequently a second group called Whitesnake, who were an offshoot from the first. To John Swallowfield was a retreat from being "on the road" constantly. Camilla meantime was attending Farlington School, at Broadbridge Heath a few miles away to the west of Horsham.

Everything was progressing happily and after taking a family photo outside of their home one summer morning in 1981 the three of them set off for Menorca for a holiday. But the peace and relaxation of their Mediterranean holiday was soon to be shattered. Not being on the telephone where they were staying, it took several hours for a message to get to them (via the local supermarket, and word of mouth) that there had been a terrible fire at Swallowfield and their home had suffered very badly. Cherie was too distraught to return, after a year of work bringing the house up to her requirements, so John went back immediately, alone.

Having surveyed the damage he phoned Cherie and Camilla from Mannings Heath to report that things were not as bad as had been feared. But he did not tell them the whole truth, Swallowfield had been very severely burnt and damaged. The fire had been so extensive it had burnt the whole of the upper part of the house, through the roof, and some of the upper floor had collapsed sending the bedroom furniture down to the family room on the ground floor. The house was, of course, uninhabitable.

The cause of the fire, which had started in the annexe, was never discovered, although there were strong suspicions of arson.

So, the distraught family moved out and lived in a portakabin-type mobile home in the courtyard whilst the builders moved in. For many months the house remained in a mess as the charred remains of the upper floor and roof were stripped out and replaced. Besides the physical destruction there was also the problem of smoke damage.

The Coletta family eventually moved back in and re-occupied Swallowfield, although much of the time was spent in London. Camilla, however, still cherished every opportunity to ride the grounds she loved so much.

In 1983 they had a call from a stranger who told Cherie, answering the door to his knock one day, that he wanted to buy their home! The caller was a brother of the Sheikh of Kuwait and his offer of £1,000,000 seemed highly attractive, especially to Cherie who had become disenchanted with Swallowfield by this time.

So the Coletta's time at Swallowfield came to an end. For Camilla the move back to London away from the lovely house and estate was heartbreaking. In the few short years the family had owned Swallowfield she had become deeply attached to it. Her memories of the happy times of her youth spent at Swallowfield did not fade with the passage of time, as one would have expected, and even now some 17 years later it still tugs at her emotionally. This is a bond that will endure, of this there can be no doubt.

The new owner of Swallowfield, the Sheikh, a member of the rich and powerful Al Sabah family, apparently flew in by helicopter for two or three weeks every summer and enjoyed the season in Sussex until, overcome by hay fever, he would fly out in and go and visit some of his many other properties around the world. When he was not in residence at Swallowfield he would leave an Indian manservant and his wife and small child on the estate to act as caretaker. They didn't occupy the house, but were accommodated in a portakabin (temporary building) adjacent to the front entrance.

Following the sudden death of his wife in 1988 the Sheikh decided to sell the property, and in 1988 the house and estate came on to the market through the London and Storrington offices of GA Property Services. The house was eventually bought by Ian and Lorely Waite, the present owners, in August 1989.

Ian, Lorely and their family were living at Shoreham-by-Sea on the Sussex coast at this time and had been planning to move since 1984. With four young children between the ages of 12 months and 14 they needed more room, in addition to which Ian was attracted to the idea of having a second (country) home where business associates could be accommodated and entertained. But a long period of searching around the environs immediately to the north of Shoreham had proved fruitless; over a dozen properties had been viewed, but none was found to be attractive.

Having reviewed Ordnance Survey maps of the area at length Ian felt that the likelihood of finding a suitable home was getting rather remote, because there really were not many homes similar to the type of property he and Lorely were looking for within a reasonable distance of Shoreham. The opportunity to build was not a viable option either, due to the lack of available land. Another alternative, to find a larger town house, also eluded them so inevitably their search was extended further afield.

When the particulars of Swallowfield first came to their attention in 1988 Ian and Lorely were unimpressed. The house was large and the grounds extensive, and it was outside the area they wished to live in. In addition, the black and white photographs in a sales brochure they were sent listing Swallowfield (and several other houses) made it appear particularly sombre and Gothic. The impression they had was of a house that was cold and uninviting.

Nothing about it seemed attractive to Ian and Lorely, including the asking price of "offers over £1,000,000", and accordingly the property was ignored. At this time Ian and Lorely felt they needed to consider the lack of space at Shoreham more urgently, and a decision was made early in 1989 to resolve the problem by extending their existing home. Having taken the decision, in principle, to extend Shoreham and use that as their primary residence, it did not seem so outlandish to then consider having a second home further away.

They had forgotten about Swallowfield when, many months later, further particulars of the property arrived one morning in the post. By this time two things had happened that had changed the situation. First, their search for a larger property had continued to be unsuccessful, and they had come to realise that the prospects of finding what they wanted in the area they had designated (within 5-10 miles of Shoreham) were likely to be negligible. Secondly, the house market had slipped and prices had fallen back from their peak. The new asking price for Swallowfield was now £800,000. These two factors prompted Lorely to suggest they take a look at Swallowfield and after making arrangements to view they set off to drive to Mannings Heath.

Unbeknown to both of them there was another factor that was to about to make a huge difference to their attitude towards the old Sussex estate of Smith Henry and Augusta Bigg - and that was the time of year. Their first visit to Swallowfield occurred on a fabulous Spring day early in May 1989, when the sun shone on a green and pleasant landscape that featured the last of the bluebells in their hosts on either side of the old drive, and early showings of magnificent rhododendrons. It was the grounds that took their breath away. As they walked around the estate they realised for the first time the extent of the woodlands and the lakes and old gardens, and they were captivated. They met Reg Elphick and his then neighbour Percy Boniface who had worked in the grounds for previous owners.

As far as the house itself was concerned their initial impressions were confirmed in every respect. It looked and felt cold and sombre, the outer sandstone walls being very grey and even black in places. It had a distinctive gloomy, Victorian appearance and was quite the opposite to the bright, spacious type of house the Waites were looking for. The accommodation was not that good either, with three principal bedrooms with en-suite facilities and two guest-rooms, with another childrens bedroom as an adjunct. An added problem was the configuration of the house, which meant that the two sets of bedrooms had to be accessed via different staircases.

Instructions had been given to local agents to sell the property and also to auction off the contents "as lying". They had decided to let prospective purchasers view the house complete with furnishings, on the basis that this would present the house to best effect, rather than for it to be viewed empty and bare. The scene that met Ian and Lorely on their inspection was quite bizarre, and was in many ways akin to a Marie-Celeste situation - it was as if the occupants had simply walked away and left, without any preparation. Of course, that is precisely what had happened, it had been abandoned. The refrigerators were still stocked with food, although much of it well past its "sell by" date. A bath was still full of water. The house was covered with a layer of accumulated dust.

The house was a daunting prospect. It had been substantially rebuilt by the Coletta's following the disastrous fire in 1981, and the work they had commissioned was undoubtedly of good quality. The house had been partially re-roofed, re-wired and re-plumbed and care had been taken to reinstate to a high standard, but over the past five years it had been poorly cared for, and now looked quite shabby and grubby. The furnishings installed by the Sheikh were not in keeping with the Victorian structure and décor, which produced a strange miss-match of styles, adding to the uncomfortable appearance of the inside of the house. However, Ian looked beyond the state of the fabric, and saw that structurally the house was sound and dry.

Further examination of the size of the estate by Ian revealed the boundaries of the property in more detail. When the Goodhews had sold Swallowfield in 1979 they had parcelled up the estate land into many packages, which had been individually bought by various purchasers; but the Coletta family had succeeded in buying back most (but not all) of those parcels of land to closely recreate the original estate, which was now up for sale.

The day's visit excited them both, but there was a drawback. When they had contacted the agent to arrange their visit the Waites had been told that the house had been sold! Apparently another party, a businessman, was very keen to buy it and had made an offer that had been accepted. Further enquiries revealed that contracts had not yet been signed. Undaunted, Ian and Lorely decided to proceed with their bid and instructed Solicitors to act for them. It then transpired that their were a number of legal problems facing any party wishing to buy the property, not the least of which was that the vendors had mislaid a key document of title - the Land Certificate. These legal difficulties had to be addressed by the respective lawyers acting for both prospective purchasers, the Waites and their rival, the businessman. It was a nerve-wracking time for all concerned as both interested purchasers and their lawyers sought to overcome the problems, or at least to minimise the risks to an acceptable level. In the end the Waites' contracts were exchanged on 14th June 1989, with completion scheduled for 8th August.

Having exchanged contract (but prior to completion) the Waites were fortunate to be able to visit Swallowfield on several occasions, as it was empty, to view the grounds more extensively and to appreciate the gardens and grounds in their summer glory. During these visits what became apparent was the extent of damage the woodlands had suffered in the great storm of 1987, and the vast amount of remedial work that would be necessary to restore the woodland rides to something close to their former state.

But the next thing immediately ahead for them was the auction of the contents of Swallowfield arranged by General Accident for 1st August 1989. The contents of the house some 326 lots were auctioned off piecemeal (by Messrs Jordan and Cook from Worthing) in a grand sale that was held under a huge marquee on the lawn outside the house. The carpets were sold as seen, lying uncleaned on the floors. All the furniture and every other piece of furnishing were identified with lot numbers. Piles of new towels and facecloths, all purchased from Harrods store in London, formed part of another lot. The garden furniture had been gathered together and arranged in a group, as if for seating an audience. Everything had to be sold and everything was sold. The auction was well attended and attracted a wide audience. The local population turned out in force, probably because it provided a longed-for chance to see for the first time inside the big, old house hidden away within the estate grounds. Buyers came from further afield attracted by the prospect of acquiring either Victorian or Arab-style furniture and fittings. Somehow the occasion got to the milling visitors. Whether it was the skill of the auctioneers, the unusual setting and circumstances, the curious collection of articles, or the excitement of bidding for such a range of large and small items will never be known, but everything was successfully sold off, and at remarkably high prices. It was almost as if those congregating at Swallowfield that day felt that they had to go away with something as a memento of the old house, whether they needed it or not, regardless of the price.

From Lorely and Ian's viewpoint this was a little frustrating as they had hoped to be able to purchase more items for the house than they did, but in many instances the prices bid were greater than the cost of buying the articles new.

One item for sale was an amphibious Argo 8-wheel All Terrain Vehicle which the previous owners had apparently used to drive into the lakes on the estate. (Reportedly they had had to be pulled out by a tractor on one occasion.)

A week later completion of the sale took place and Lorely and Ian arrived to take possession of the keys from the agents. They were amazed at the transformation that met their eyes. From the hub-bub of the auction only a few days earlier, when the house had been full of furniture, furnishings and people, now it was bare and desolate. (So bare in fact that even some of the items they had bought in the auction had disappeared). Extraordinarily, however, the house looked better for being devoid of its contents (which in many respects had seemed misplaced) and even the estate agent commented that, had he appreciated how much better it appeared empty, he would have sold it on that basis.

After celebrating their achievement in buying Swallowfield, Ian and Lorely paid another visit to Mannings Heath to see once again what they had bought and to decide what they needed to do to the property. This time the sun was not shining and again they were faced with the sombre-looking house, and the prospect of years of work to transform it into the family home they wanted. The first decision was relatively easy; they would not immediately embark upon a large-scale programme of re-modelling and refurbishment, but would occupy it as a second home and use it for weekends and holidays whilst they took stock of what they wanted to do.

With the house stripped Ian's view was confirmed, the structure was sound and it afforded a solid base on which to plan for the future. In short order rooms were cleaned and furnishings put in from Shoreham so that in its part-furnished state it could be used on a temporary basis. A burglar alarm system was also installed.

A few weeks later a housewarming party was scheduled to tie in with Bonfire Night. The weather was kind and allowed a splendid evening's celebration to take place, with well over 100 people being entertained. In addition to a magnificent fireworks display, the traditional bonfire offered the perfect way of disposing of some of the fallen timber from the 1987 storm. During 1990 many happy occasions took place at Swallowfield. Numerous weekend house-parties, holiday breaks, and get-togethers were held allowing friends and family to be entertained. Favourite outdoor activities seemed to be clay pigeon shooting and, for the youngsters, ATV riding and fishing. Whenever appropriate, the fitter guests were encouraged to turn their hands to the benefit of the estate and, typically, logging parties would help to clear fallen timber and re-open the woodland rides. After one such effort in the early months of 1990 Ian woke after a stormy winter's night to be faced with what appeared to be twice as many fallen trees as there had been the previous evening! This setback was offset by the discovery of a long-lost lily pond hidden away amongst the overgrown rhododendron - which then became another restoration project for sometime in the future.

Among other events not so entertaining were the occasions when the burglar alarm was activated in the middle of the night, requiring a prompt response from Ian or Lorely at Shoreham, along with the local police. On one such occasion the Waites arrived at Swallowfield in the dead of night, with the police, after the alarm had been triggered, to find no obvious sign of a break in, but to be puzzled by the alarm system log which showed "something" had tripped 11 alarm sensors in succession, as if "it" was walking around the house. Quite a remarkable feat, really, as all the doors remained locked. No one, not even the police or the security company could explain that one.

Plans for re-furbishing and altering the house gradually evolved in Ian's mind over the next few months. Some of the ideas were based on practical necessity, whereas others were longer term, more extensive schemes. Amongst the first things to be done was a scheme to change the upstairs accommodation, to link the bedroom access at upper floor level without the need to use separate staircases. This was seen to be essential by Lorely to give ready access and communication with all bedrooms. But even this project had complications and was not straightforward; a number of levels were involved, and the space had to be used to good effect. Another wish was to do away with the sunroom (which had started off its life as a conservatory). Above all, however, was the priority to ensure the shell of the building was sound and the services and utilities were in good order. It seemed that a programme of works needed to be mapped out to fit all these ideas into an orderly plan that could then be tackled in phases.

Having thoroughly enjoyed Swallowfield during 1990, the Waites decided to spend Christmas there and yet again the weekend logging parties were to continue into 1991.

However, having formulated various ideas for remodelling the house, a commitment was made to proceed. The decision was taken in 1991 to employ a firm of architects to develop designs, draw up specifications, call for tenders, let contracts and manage the various activities. After a careful selection process an appointment was made. At this juncture Ian's approach was to stand away and to let the professionals manage the letting and supervision of the works as they progressed step by step. This would be a better use of his time, and would enable him to concentrate on his business interests.

Unfortunately things did not proceed according to plan. It took some six months for the initial schemes to be worked up, having in the meantime also obtained useful information from the architects who had worked on Swallowfield for the Coletta family. By December 1991 Ian was advised that dimension surveys were needed and then drawings would have to be made from those surveys. It was not until February/March 1992 that sketches were finally reviewed with a view to a scheme being adopted. By July and August plans had been submitted to the local parish and district councils and were approved by October that year. During the following five months tender specifications were prepared and issued, with responses not being received until the end of March 1993 - almost two years after the decision to proceed. When the bids did arrive they were all in excess of the budget that had been set; not marginally, but by several multiples!

Outside of this construction planning activity, social activities and functions were carried out as frequently and with as much enthusiasm as possible. Birthday celebrations, weekend house parties, and summer events were organised to make maximum advantage of the weather and use of the grounds. The installation of an all-weather tennis court in 1991 was popular, but cricket, bowls, croquet and similar games were also played by guests - sometimes at night as well as by day. "School gatherings" took place from time to time, with one event involving thirty-three 13-14 year olds of both sexes staying for a weekend. What Ian and Lorely hadn't counted on was the need for them to patrol the corridors all night to ensure respectable behaviour!

Planning activity from April 1993 to February 1994 eventually produced a firm to whom a contract to build was let; albeit yet again the tenders had come in with prices far in excess of what they had been led to believe was realistic. Revised plans were drafted and approval obtained, only for the firm in question to walk away from the contract some seven months later. It was back to the start line again.

During this period it had been suggested to Ian that he should re-use re-constituted stone in the new building work at Swallowfield, because the original source at Winterpit Lane (the quarry) was no longer available, itself having been developed. A study of geological maps of the area had to be made in an attempt to find a matching sandstone in the local area, but to no avail. The search took over 3 months and involved the help of the National Geological Society. It even extended to quarries in France and Germany. In the end a very satisfactory sandstone was traced in Yorkshire, with the added advantage that it was harder than the original, and would therefore last longer before deteriorating - some 400 years life expectancy was quoted.

Towards the end of 1994 and into early 1995 Ian was to engage in a final and third round of tendering at Swallowfield, but to no avail. Ian and Lorely felt it was time to take stock and consider alternative approaches to getting the works done. Ian reviewed construction activities of a similar size and scope to their project at Swallowfield that were being undertaken in the locality. He was aware of the reconstruction of the nearby local manor house, called Fullers, which was being developed as the new Mannings Heath Golf Clubhouse, and contacted the owners to enquire about the way they had approached the scheme. Introductions were made to an architect, Peter Smart, and in December 1995 Peter was engaged to start work on the Swallowfield project. Ian felt a fresh start and a clean drawing board were what was needed, and Peter's brief was to develop new plans and to secure the necessary consents.

Unfortunately, over the decades Swallowfield had been extended and added to in a piecemeal fashion, and was an uncoordinated assembly of rooms, floors, roof lines and levels - as well as suffering from lack of care and maintenance. In short, the only thing to do was to "square up" and balance the outside of the house, and to re-organise the interior to provide a sensible layout and order.

Due to past activities Ian already had a firm idea of what he wanted to achieve, which he now undertook in phases, rather than to try and do everything at once; this would also enable him to maintain a closer grip on things as they progressed. This was a difficult time as he was still extremely active in his business interests.

Between January and April 1996 plans were drawn up, revised, agreed and submitted to Horsham District Council for approval. These plans entailed the re-modelling of the south-east elevation. Planning Approval was obtained in May.

This phase would see the demolition of the old sun-room (ex conservatory) and downstairs cloakroom. In their place on the ground floor a full-sized snooker room, incorporating an open fire and bar, would be built. The master bedroom above would also disappear and in its place would appear a new first floor in this area of the building linking the existing first floor areas at the front and back of the house. This would provide a further two bedrooms and three bathrooms. An extension to the rear staircase would then lead to a second games room, which would be hidden away within the new gables; and centrally an existing staircase leading to a tank room would be re-modelled to provide a sitting room/dressing room, as an adjunct to the master bedroom.

As an immediate second stage the old generator and boiler rooms externally were to be replaced by a new boiler house to match the size and shape of the existing utility room

It was a condition of the planning consent that the colour and texture of the materials used matched those of the existing, details having to be agreed with the West Sussex's Chief Architect. In addition to this detail, Ian also required that the joinery should be of the highest quality, and match the design of the existing house. Accordingly, plans envisaged the use of Sapele Mahogany for the windows, even though they were to be painted, and Douglas Fir timber for the barge-boards. Natural slate tiling for the pitched roofs was also specified.

When Peter and Ian met the WSCC architect to show him the plans they had a surprise in store. Thinking he would be delighted with the standards specified and the materials to be used (which he was), they were somewhat taken aback when he commented that perhaps rather than faithfully reproduce the Victorian design they should put a 20th century statement on the building, by designing something much more modern and radical.

A last house party was held in July 1996, prior to commencing the demolition and re-build; a grand occasion with some 200 guests in attendance.

Construction commenced in August and by year-end foundations had been laid and the ground floor and stonework to the walls was being effected. Wherever possible existing stonework taken down from the windows, gable ends or from the base of the old conservatory, was stored and re-used. It has been particularly pleasing to see the different colours in this removed stonework, sometimes a delicate pink blush, on other pieces a soft grey hue, and to observe it reappearing somewhere in the restored Swallowfield. Already the new sandstone is merging with the old to perpetuate the appearance of a Victorian grand house of distinction. With all new additions being constructed in this sandstone, and the existing stone cleaned to restore its original colour the result is both impressive and pleasing to the eye. As Ian has commented, the Victorians did not build "grey" houses, they were much more colourful when new.

As physical construction was taking place on the main house extension in 1997, Lorely and Ian determined their requirements for the next phase, namely the "garage extension" as it became known, and Peter drew up plans which were agreed that June.

This second phase would provide accommodation on the ground floor for six cars and a cloakroom, with access to the existing commercial kitchen below ground floor level in the existing house. On the first floor there would be two bedrooms, two bathrooms, a study and main living room area complete with a vaulted ceiling and minstrels gallery. To top it off, a clock tower would be erected, with clock faces on two aspects and a weather vane designed by Ian as a flight of swallows.

Again, all materials had to match faithfully the existing in design, colour, quality and texture. In addition the refurbishment of the existing house started to take on another dimension as Ian felt that the condition of certain parts of the fabric should be upgraded too, replacing all existing barge-boards on the twenty-two gables. Groundwork on the garage extension started around the autumn of 1997, but problems arose that resulted in a setback of almost two years.

Whereas the house when purchased by the Waites had been dry and watertight, the work that was subsequently carried out on constructing the new garage wing resulted in a key part of the drainage system running under the basement rooms of the house being blocked. The workmen had unearthed a drainage pipe and not realising its significance had sealed it off. Unbeknown to everyone at the time, there was a network of Victorian land drains running below Swallowfield and these now ceased to function. As a result, the basement became very damp as water was not carried away, but retained in the foundations. Eventually the damp damaged the basement structure, spread up the walls of the basement to ground floor level and started to effect areas that had already been refurbished. When the problem was identified it required yet another major programme of works to solve it. With the problem corrected the commercial kitchen (largely consisting of stainless steel work surfaces and fittings suitable to support a medium size hotel) was reinstated, the old wine cellar was refurbished, and the music room converted into a soundproofed entertainment room, or mini-cinema, for films to be shown or music played at volumes that would rock the old house to its foundations.

In the Spring of 1998 Ian and Lorely had agreed with Peter Smart the final details of the new Orangery that was to be built on the south face of the old house, alongside the drawing rooms. This would provide an extension of the formal drawing rooms and the doubling of space in the area; in addition, it would feature a dramatic entrance on to the lawned gardens via a new terrace that Ian had in mind. The Orangery was to be of classic design, constructed in stone, but with Gothic fanlights reflecting the Victorian era. To complete the design a balustraded veranda over the Orangery would be accessible from both the master and adjacent bedrooms. From here one could take advantage of wonderful uninterrupted views across the parkland and down to the woodlands by the lakes.

Accordingly, plans were finalised and approved by Horsham District Council, with a view to starting construction as soon as practicable after the garage extension was completed.

By the autumn of 1998 the shell of the garage block was largely completed, but Ian was becoming increasingly concerned about not being on-site frequently enough to oversee matters to the extent that he felt he should. In addition, the basement flooding problem had not been resolved at that juncture, and it was becoming more difficult to work around that situation. Furthermore, there were other works that Ian wanted to effect as soon as possible, like the Orangery and Terrace.

The decision Ian and Lorely then took was that Ian would take over in person the role of Clerk of Works, as a full-time commitment, until the works were finished and the family had moved in. This was a major change and one that was not taken lightly. The advantages that were anticipated principally revolved around two issues. In the first place Ian was convinced that he needed to be on hand to monitor all trades and organisations working at Swallowfield to ensure that the agreed plans and specifications were carried out to the letter, and that they were making on-the-spot decisions in keeping with the overall design. (There had been an on-going concern that compromises were being made all too often.) Secondly, Ian felt that being on-hand on a daily basis would help overall progress of the works. Being on the spot enabled decisions to be made promptly, both in respect of anticipating future needs and to pronounce on how problems should be overcome. So that is what happened, and from that time forward things steadily got better. Hindsight is a wonderful thing and Ian wishes he had taken the decision from the outset, without having to suffer years of frustration and delays, but unfortunately it's a gift that none of us are blessed with.

A further advantage of Ian being permanently at Swallowfield whilst the work has been going on has been that his mind has been continually working on further schemes and ideas for improving and altering the building, such that modifications have been possible here and there as the various trades have carried out their work. This has often resulted in slight changes (and sometimes major ones) as work has been progressed which, although pleasing to Ian, have no doubt given risen on occasions to many quiet asides and pleas to the heavens by the workforce. Ian freely admits that what has started as one thing has led to another, and what was drawn up in the plans is not strictly what appears before the eyes. (But this being said, all works have been meticulously carried out in conformity with planning laws and building regulations.)

Yet another of Ian's schemes around this time involved work on the Victorian kitchen garden wall. As ever, he went to great lengths to ensure a perfect match in the design and colour of the materials used. The wall itself represented the fourth side of a quarter-acre garden, and would provide the necessary enclosure to ensure that animals such as rabbits and deer could not enter the vegetable garden that Ian intended to restore. Construction of the wall started in October, along with the building of a small stone wall by the main house. When the job was finished some 26,000 bricks had been used - enough to construct three reasonably sized homes!

Ian's attention was geared to two other things at this time, namely clearing the tracks around the perimeter of the woodland, and getting ready for the groundwork on the Orangery for an early start in the new year - weather permitting. Working with contractors, Ian spent over a month clearing the arboretum, the dead pines felled in 1987 near to the lakes, and clearing the main rides through the woods. At that time he saw the opportunity to extend the lakes to improve the fishing and general amenity use. Another project awaits!

In early January 1999 groundwork started on the Orangery and progress moved along quite rapidly. In addition, initial groundwork started on the courtyard. By Spring most of the structure was in place, and internal refurbishment or second fixings to new work was taking place where it could, bearing in mind the basement flooding problem had yet to be cleared. The water well had been checked out in the courtyard and an automatic pump installed to provide water for the kitchen garden in times of drought.

The courtyard work was ready to start in earnest with some 30,000 granite sets being shipped from Portugal for the project, which would take six months to complete. Immediately thereafter work commenced on the terrace, working round from the courtyard to the front of the house. This required some 400 square metres of stone being hauled down from another Yorkshire quarry. At the same time, sandstone walls of the terrace were being built leading down to the landscaped lawns that Ian was to seed himself in October.

September had been completely rained off, not allowed any work on the lawns to take place, but there was good news on the basement front. Ian discovered the blocked drain himself, prior to his appointing an hydrologist, and at last corrective work could be put in hand to fix the problem. It also meant that remedial work could be considered in earnest for those areas of the house that had been affected by the damp.

During the course of the year 2000 a major effort was made to concentrate on finishing the bulk of the internal refurbishment work in the main house, in order to catch up on some of the lost time.

What has resulted from all the work carried out over the past four and a half years has been remarkable. Whilst the building has been re-modelled, restyled, extended and altered what has evolved is a new Swallowfield. It may look quite different from the house that Smith Henry Bigg and his wife built, but it has been carefully changed in keeping with the original concept. It still retains its Victorian style, but it is bright and colourful, having lost the sombre, dark appearance created through the passage of time.

External improvements also include Welsh slate roofing, new iron down-pipes and decorated barge-boards all to match the originals. Concealed low-voltage sodium lighting will also be fitted to provide soft illumination of the gables at night, in addition to security lighting. The dining room bay window in stone has been completely rebuilt, including a new timber window and shutters to match the original.

To cater for increased power loads the electricity feeds have been enhanced and a state-of-the-art heating system on a grand scale ensures that all bathrooms and kitchens can be simultaneously supplied with endless quantities of piping hot water. External utility cables have been re-routed underground and the surface and foul drainage systems completely renewed.

Internally the changes are considerable. Every room has been totally refurbished and many alterations carried out to make the home easier to live in and more comfortable, and to make the best use of space. The house has so many levels, staircases and turns it is quite easy to get lost, but every twist and turn reveals something exciting, whether it's a clever use of space, the quality of some restored woodwork, or the beauty of a plaster cornice.

All along the intention has been to rebuild the house as a home for the Waite family to occupy, and not to think of its potential commercially. And that's one of the reasons why, in the high roof space among the beams and trusses, and covered by a large skylight designed to be hidden from view at ground level, can be found a light and airy games room of enormous dimensions.

Some decisions still have to be made on the interior décor and furnishings, but these are being postponed for the time being, so that Lorely and Ian can muse for longer before opting finally on these important issues. Initially some of the older furniture will be used, but the family is reconciled to the fact that most furniture will have to be new. It is possible that some rooms may be decorated and furnished in Victorian style, but we will have to wait and see. The quality of plasterwork, woodwork and cornices during the rebuild has been particularly high, and a decision on whether walls will remain painted, or will be papered, is also being left for the time being.

Once the family is safely settled in their new home, Ian will be planning the next scheme no doubt. Still to be tackled is the Victorian canopy, coach house and stable block and the two drives. And out in the grounds there are thoughts about creating a track around the boundary of the estate to allow access by vehicles. The area in front of the main entrance to the house also needs attention, as it has suffered whilst years of building works have been going on. But here there is the prospect of creating a distinctive frontage for Swallowfield by some sympathetic landscaping, perhaps designed around a turning-sweep enclosing a fountain. And then there is the kitchen garden to tackle, and many, many more ideas...........

And at last, some eleven and a half years after the house was purchased, the Waite family eventually moved in to Swallowfield in December 2000. There is still much to be done but Lorely was better placed than Augusta Bigg when she and Smith Henry made their move in to the house in 1845, at least she had windows, doors and a WC.

Swallowfield from the south aspect, circa 1930. Note the rose beds laid in the lawn. *Photo - Allen Flint*

The entrance hall of Swallowfield, probably in the 1930s.

Another interior view, taken at the same time as the photo above.

The west aspect of Swallowfield in August 1991. *Photo - Ian Waite*

Again July 1991, showing the sun-room on the south-east corner. *Photo - Ian Waite*

The view from the upper floor of the lawns and woodlands, in 1993. Note the pattern of the old rose beds.
Photo - Ian Waite

The walled kitchen garden as it was in 1993. *Photo - Ian Waite*

One of the beautiful lakes at Swallowfield on a chilly autumn morning in 1993, still bearing the marks of the 1987 storm and sadly lacking care. *Photo - Ian Waite*

The woods that were once so splendidly maintained also show years of neglect. (1992) *Photo - Ian Waite*

The old entrance drive to Swallowfield, leading off the Horsham - Cowfold road (now the A281), decked in bluebells. Spring 1999. *Photo -Tony Turner*

An original oak panelled door at Swallowfield. *Photo - Ian Waite*

Victorian tiling still evident in the kitchen passageway in 1999. *Photo - Tony Turner*

Some of the original beams exposed were originally ship's timbers. This iron hook and eye was used as a method of attaching and securing beams.
Photo - Ian Waite

The main approach to Swallowfield, along the old driveway, as it appeared in 1993. Work has yet to start on the old house. *Photo - Ian Waite*

Before and after -1.Before work on the south-east wing is started. *Photo - Ian Waite*

Before and after -2. Taking down the south-east wing, August 1996. *Photo - Ian Waite*

Before and after - 3. The new two-storey wing goes up, and matches the existing two gables 1997.
Photo - Ian Waite

The Orangery with its ballustraded veranda is in its finishing stages, the terrace is laid, and the steps to the new lowered lawn are going in. Autumn 1999. *Photo - Ian Waite*

Winter 1999 and the re-modelling of south aspect nears completion. *Photo - Tony Turner*

Another "before and after" sequence.
The courtyard as it was at the end of 1997, when the garage extension was underway. *Photo - Ian Waite*

And how it looked as the last of the granite sets were being laid. *Photo - Ian Waite*

The new appearance of Swallowfield starts to take shape in 2000. The garage extension is to the left of the tree.
Photo - Tony Turner

Chapter Ten
The Church of the Good Shepherd

The little church that Smith Henry's daughter Augusta had built in memory of her brother William remains a cherished part of the heritage of Mannings Heath and has been lovingly kept and maintained over the years. Built of red brick, it consists of just the principal nave, a small chancel canopied in Gothic style under a stone arch and a minute vestry, no more than 2 metres by 1 metre, curtained off to one side of the chancel. Above the steeply pitched, tiled roof is a bell in a small white-painted bell-cote.

Behind the small altar is the wonderful stained-glass window, mentioned in Chapter 4, made of two lights separated by a mullion. The left-hand window portrays a shepherd and his sheep, whilst the right-hand depicts Christ the Good Shepherd. The window constitutes the whole of the east wall. Separating the chancel from the nave is a carved communion rail, with central twin-hinging doors. Over the altar is a brass lamp suspended by three chains. The walls internally are unrendered brick above shoulder height, painted a pale yellow. The roof is of trussed wood construction.

In the small entrance porch are two brass war memorial plaques that were originally fitted to the Wesleyan Chapel (built in 1869) at one end of the village green, and 'rescued' when it was subsequently converted to a house.

The church sits in a plot of land which itself measures only a little over 10m x 16.5m (28′ x 46′), so the church is a tight fit. As part of the parish of Nuthurst, services are conducted at the Church of the Good Shepherd (or COGS as it is known colloquially by the Parish choir) every week, to serve the growing population of the village. Although originally fitted with chairs in Augusta's time, pews were brought in subsequently from Copsale church. There are nine pews at present, so if each sits five (at a pinch), the capacity is approximately 45 souls.

Allen Flint lived in Mannings Heath from a boy and has written down his recollections of the church and the village:-

"In 1920 there still lived at Mannings Heath the two members of the Bigg family who built the Church of the Good Shepherd in memory of their parents in the year 1881.

Major Frederick Bigg lived and farmed at Swallowfield and also owned Cooks estate at Nuthurst (opposite St. Andrew's Church.) His sister, Miss Augusta Bigg, lived at Ryecroft. She was an elderly lady but she still attended the church regularly. Her mode of transport was an ancient wicker Bath chair pulled by one of her gardeners, and escorted by two elderly maids by the surname Moulding.

The Church at that time was lit, as were all the houses, by paraffin lamps. Four lamps were suspended from the roof of the nave, one hung at the side of the pulpit, an oil lantern hung in the porch and the chancel was lit by candles. Heating was by means of an open coal fire. This was situated directly opposite the door and the font stood in front of it. The font and fire have long since gone.

The seating arrangements were long wooden forms, or benches, and a few chairs. The aisle was covered with a length of coconut matting, and a red carpet square covered the chancel. The communion rails were plain iron railings and, looking towards the chancel, the pulpit was on the wall at the right hand side.

On the other side was the pedal organ, played by a Miss Reading. She had already played for many years and went on to complete 50 years and more. The Church caretaker was the wife of the village blacksmith, Mark Brister. The collection was taken by Mr Dancy, Head Gardener at Swallowfield. He used to lead the singing in a powerful tenor. When he died in 1946, his funeral service was held in the church.

Among the congregation in the early '20s was a very old lady who lived near the Wesleyan Chapel, by the name of Hannah Wickens and three spinster ladies by the name of Ellis. The oldest of them was Headmistress of the village school. She was known to the pupils as Granny Ellis. Two other members of the congregation were the Misses Mason, who kept the little general shop in Pound Lane.

We had our own curate at the time who lived in the village. One was the Reverend Allen who formed a troop of Scouts and also collected a substantial sum of money to enable Will Thorns, a local crippled man, to go to a London hospital for an operation. Will Thorns later became the village cobbler and it was he who built the present village stores.

Another curate we had was the Reverend Huxtable. One year he had arranged for all the ex-Servicemen to attend an evening service on November 11th. He had a bugler play the Last Post and Reveille in the church porch. The church was packed that night and afterwards he laid on a supper and a concert in the village hall, then known as the Drill Hall because it had originally been built for the Church Lad's Brigade.(This is not the present village hall, which is a much more recent structure.)

Later the curate offended many people because of the posters he put up outside the church. One read "Don't be a Mannings Heathen, but be a Christian and come to Church". Another read "Come to Church for Christ's sake". He suffered a nervous breakdown and went away. Soon afterwards the rector, the Reverend Packenham-Gilbert died and we had no more curates in Mannings Heath.

The village, in those days of nearly 70 years ago, was totally different to what it is today.

In addition to the Church, there was a well attended Wesleyn Chapel, a village school, with three teachers and around 70 pupils, a village hall, which housed a Working Men's Club, and later on a Women's Institute. We also had two Sunday Schools, a troop of Scouts and both cricket and football teams. There were at that time three shops, a blacksmiths forge and a village cobbler. Until the 1914-1918 war there were two public houses, the Dun Horse and the Ingleside. We had a Post Office, and the law was enforced by P.C.Clapp.

Everyone worked in or around the village on farms or estates, or were employed locally, timber felling or well digging. At Monks Gate there was a builders and undertaking business.

Many of the cottages were "tied" i.e they went with the job. Private cottages were let at around 5 shillings (25p) per week. Wages were around 30 shillings (£1.50) per week with Head Gardeners and the like about £2. Everyone grew their own vegetables, many kept a few chickens, and quite a few had a pig down the garden.

Milk was fetched from the farms before we went to school, but later was brought to the door in cans. Coal was delivered by horse and cart, at around 1/10d (about 9p) per hundredweight and nearly every cottager had his stack of cord-wood and faggots.

Houses were lit by oil lamps and candles for there was no electricity, neither was there television or wireless, and only about three or four cars in the village and, until about 1923, there were no buses.

All funerals were held at Nuthurst, and often a wagon and pair of horses did service as a hearse, with the mourners walking. All blinds would be drawn in the house along the route till the cortege had passed.

I joined the Church Choir at Nuthurst in 1921, walking there and back each Sunday. Many years before that, in the early 1800s, my Great Grandfather had played the Bass Viol in the Minstrel's Gallery, before the organ was installed."

The Church of The Good Shepherd is set in a very small parcel of land, so that the wall of the church bearing the main stained-glass window is only a few feet from the pavement of Church Road. As Mannings Heath gradually expands and new houses are added in small developments from time to time, the little church that Augusta had built in memory of her beloved younger brother William, still remains to serve the spiritual needs of the local community. Augusta would be pleased about that, and to know that it is so cherished by the Parish and its people.

Interior of the Church of the Good Shepherd circa 1994. *Photo - Tony Turner*

Exterior of the Church of the Good Shepherd circa 1994. *Photo - Tony Turner*

PART THREE

From Part One of the Story of Swallowfield we have seen that none of the five children of Smith Henry Bigg and his wife Augusta was successful in continuing the Bigg line, except for Henry. It will be recalled that Henry, the eldest son, went to Australia as a young man, married Annie and had three children, two boys Frederick and Alfred and a daughter Amy. Frederick had died at the age of three, and when we left them at the end of Chapter 3, Alfred and Amy had both married. We will now pick up their stories and follow their lives and the lives of their descendants to establish a continuous link to the present day. Because we will be covering several generations, it will have to be done with some brevity.

In this section we will also learn what happened to the two Australian properties Swallowfield NSW and Thalgarrah.

Part Three

Chapter Eleven
Henry's Descendants in Australia

When in 1856 Henry Bigg's mother and father (Augusta and Smith Henry) first mooted to him the idea of going to live and work at Salisbury Court, near Uralla in New South Wales, it must have conjured up many pictures in his mind. The name Salisbury Court certainly had an important ring to it. We don't know what information Mrs Marsh imparted to Augusta about Salisbury Court, or the area round Uralla, but probably it was limited. Would Henry have been told that he would be farming at an altitude of around 3,000 ft, because that is precisely what he would be doing on his arrival and for many years afterwards. To someone living in the United Kingdom any land over 3,000ft is thought of as mountainous, so it might have been unsettling to tell Henry that piece of information about the area around Uralla. In fact the Northern Tablelands around the Armidale district of New England, where Uralla is situated, is a high plateau featuring gentle rolling hills with not a mountain in sight. The only clues to its altitude are what look like prodigious cracks in the ground on the eastern side, on the escarpment, caused by erosion as the rivers flow to the coastal plain below. These cracks result in massive gorges and spectacular waterfalls.

The gorge at Dangars Falls, not far from Uralla, a 120m drop. *Photo - Tony Turner*

Originally the district was aboriginal country, but after early explorers pushed up into the New England area in the period 1815-1818 and reported favourable conditions for settlers, it wasn't long before squatters moved with their sheep beyond the boundaries of the State's protection, despite restrictions on this practice from the government of the day.

After a law was passed in 1836 that allowed free men to have a licence and as much land as they wanted, anywhere, for just a nominal fee, the pace of settler activity understandably quickened considerably. By 1839 Armidale was a small slab and bark village, with a few stores and an inn. It started as an administration centre and was named by Commissioner MacDonald of the border police after his father's baronial estate in England. Over the next 10 years Armidale grew to the size of a town with some two hundred and fifty buildings, the majority of them still being constructed of timber.

A few years prior to Henry becoming interested in the area gold was found at several locations, including Rocky River to the north of Uralla, and within 5 years 5,000 people had rushed to the area hoping to cash in on the discovery. The boom years on the Rocky River were between 1856 and 1859. (See map in chapter 3.)

Uralla is known as Thunderbolt Country, after events that occurred between 1863 and 1870. Captain Thunderbolt was the name a notorious bushranger of the period gave himself. Escaping from Cockatoo Island in Sydney Harbour in September 1863, where he was serving a 10 year sentence for horse stealing, Frederick Ward - to give him his real name - spent the next 6½ years robbing mail coaches, roadside inns, stores, and homesteads in the district, and even held up the entire township of Quirindi. He met his end in a furious shoot-out with Constable Walker in May 1870, and both men are remembered by memorials in Uralla's main street. Constable Walker is commemorated with a plaque, whereas Thunderbolt astride his horse is recreated in a life-sized bronze statue.

The first property that Henry and Annie bought was 3km south of Uralla (itself 23km to the south west of Armidale.) It was a block near to a popular venue, the racecourse, which had a lagoon in the middle of it. It will be recalled that one of Henry's schemes was to sell watermelons to the punters at the racecourse. The English trees he planted between the house and the lagoon are still a feature of the landscape.

Later in life, when he had been through all the trials and tribulations we have heard about in Chapter 3, Henry received a settlement of money from his parents in 1877, and subsequently benefited from inheritances as other relatives died. These enabled him and his family to raise their standard of living considerably. In 1878 he bought 23,000 acres 17km north-east of Armidale, and called it Thalgarrah.

Where the name Thalgarrah came from is not known, and because it did not appear on any early maps, the chances are that Henry gave the name to his new grazing property. It seems to be a combination of European and Aboriginal words. "Thal" (or "Tal") comes from the German for valley. As for "garrah", the local river is the Gara, and there is a town to the north of Armidale by the name of Guyra, from an Aboriginal word for "fish can be caught".

Thalgarrah was built on high ground above the River Gara (see diagram overleaf) Between the house and the river was a natural depression, fed by a stream known as the "back gully", which flowed from a ridge to the north-west. The outlet from the depression was dammed, causing a lake to be formed below the homestead. This was deepened at the southern end to provide a facility for washing sheep before shearing, which was the practice in the late 1880s. Washing cut the weight of the wool bales thereby reducing transport costs.

In due course, between the lake and the Gara River Henry would plant many English trees, and create a garden and an orchard. This was to become an unusual feature in the open landscape, contrasting with the natural vegetation of the Northern Tablelands - grassland, scrub, and gum trees, such as stringybark and blackbutt. In this way Henry recreated a piece of his Sussex homeland on Thalgarrah and left a lasting tribute to the Sussex countryside where he spent many of his early years as a young boy. The colours of the trees in the autumn still attract many artists and photographers each year.

The Thalgarrah property was divided in 1888 when Henry and Annie gave some 500 acres (two paddocks) on the north of the Rockville road and east of the river to daughter Amy and her husband, Henry Welch Curtis, as a wedding present. The young couple added it to their existing property and then built a home they called Brooklyn, which looked down towards Thalgarrah.

Two years later, in 1890, when their son Alfred married Mabel Spasshatt, daughter of an Armidale doctor, Henry and Annie did not transfer another part of their remaining property to the newlyweds, but instead built a new home for them on high ground across the Gara River, to the east of a natural lagoon, in what was known as the East Paddock of Thalgarrah. The lagoon was of a large but shallow expanse of water lying in a natural fold in the land supplied by a gully coming in from the east. Water for the house was taken from rainwater tanks, with the surplus run into an underground tank and pumped up (by a hand pump) to a small header tank above the laundry and bathroom. Alfred and Mabel's new home was called Swallowfield, after his father's home in Sussex, and was a four-roomed wooden house surrounded by large verandas.

At the same time, a workman's cottage was built to the east and the first occupants were Bob and Alice Hoy. Between this house and Swallowfield horse stables, cow bails, and yards were built above a small dam for watering the stock.

There was no wedding gift of land to Alfred because father and son ran Thalgarrah together, and Alfred would inherit the whole property on his father's death.

So the three families - Henry and Annie Bigg, and their two adult children and their spouses all came to live in adjacent properties as neighbours. (But as we have already heard in Chapter 3, the last of the selectors was not bought out by Henry Bigg until 1894, or thereabouts, so it was not until then that Thalgarrah was wholly occupied by the Bigg family.) Henry and Annie lived at Thalgarrah, Alfred and Mabel lived at Swallowfield, and Amy and Henry Welch Curtis lived at Brooklyn.

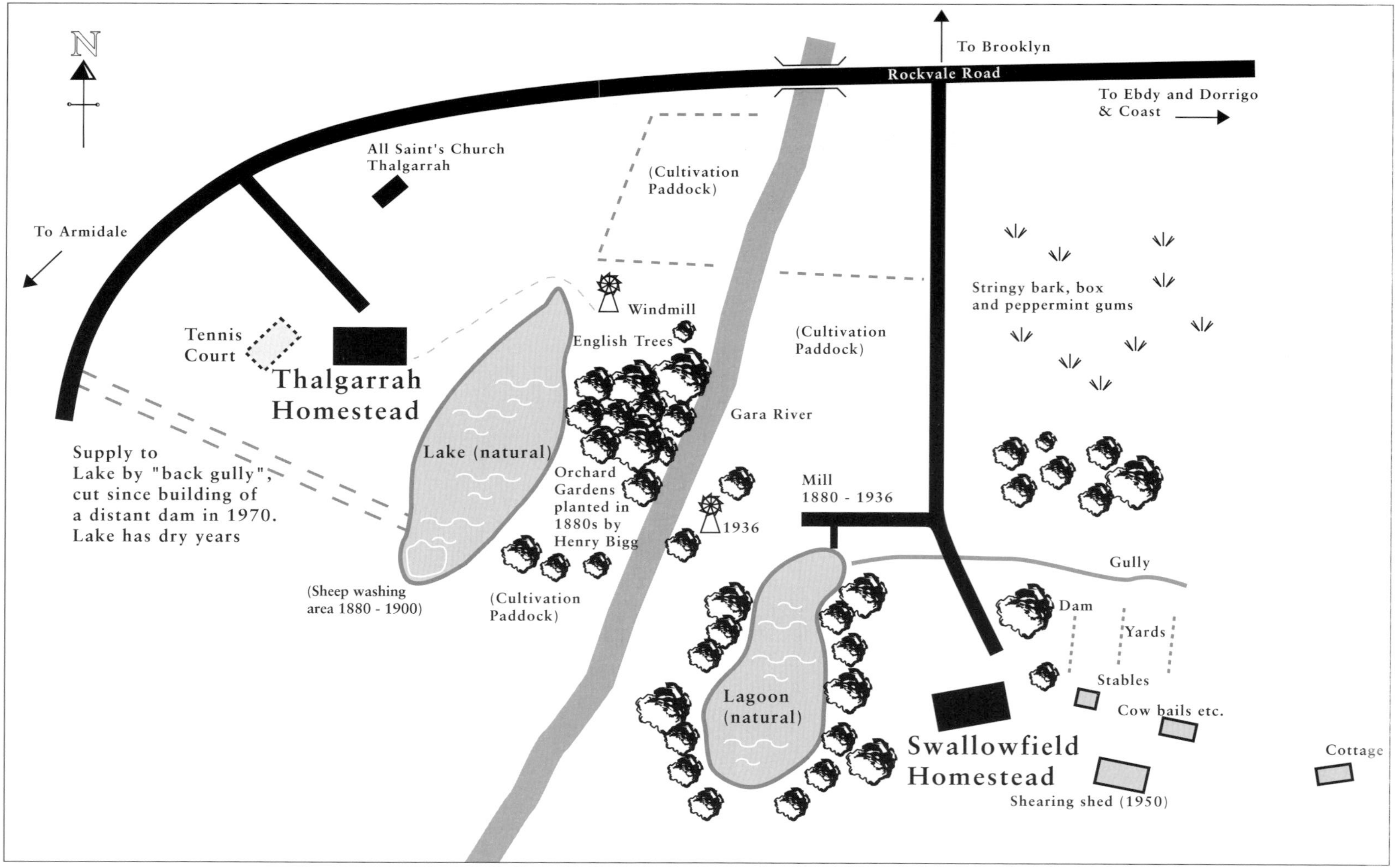

Diagram showing relationship of Thalgarrah and Swallowfield NSW.

Tony Turner

Let us now pick up the stories of the two children of Henry and Annie who lived beyond childhood, Alfred and Amy. (Young Frederick, their firstborn, had died of diphtheria at the age of three.)

Alfred Edward (born 1862)

Although Alfred's parents, Henry and Annie, had gone through very tough times it was probably still an enjoyable life for him growing up as a youngster. He had a pony of his own, won prizes at the Uralla Show, enjoyed fishing and shooting and helping his father, whilst at the same time obtaining a good grounding at the local school. He was strongly left-handed but was made to write right-handed. The result was a very neat script, but he continued to be left-handed in everything else.

When the family returned from England with their new-found wealth, in July 1877, Alfred was quickly enrolled at Sydney Grammar - that same month, in fact. During the next 18 months it is recorded that "Bigg's Cadet Rifles team won prizes". He spent mid-terms and short holidays with the Harold Burnells at Darlinghurst, and with the Tom Barkers at Maryland, Bringelly. [22]

Alfred left Sydney Grammar School after only 18 months, presumably because all available money was needed for buying property and building Thalgarrah, and because his labour was needed on the property, which was virtually virgin bush. He was not academically inclined, so at the age of only 16 years it seemed sensible for him to return home to learn at first hand the management side of his future inheritance. There is a family story that he and a friend set up a chaff-cutting business, sometimes at Thalgarrah, and occasionally travelling around the district.

On 27th May 1885, at the age of 22, we find him setting off on a "Gentleman's Grand Tour" of the world on the P & O steamer "Clyde".[23] He went to England and stayed for some while with his relatives at Swallowfield and The Hyde, where he had a horse set aside for his use. He was conscientious in his duty to write home, telling his family the important matters concerning his trip - such as the shooting trips he had been out on and the guns he had used. He also wrote in great detail of the excitement surrounding his Uncle Fred's marriage to Rose Curtis. So much so that his father complimented him on his description of the dresses *"which interested Amy and Lucy to the last degree"*. (Uncle Fred was his father's youngest brother Frederick.)

He returned to Australia in March 1886 and always told his father that it was on one of the last passenger sailing ships to round The Horn, and how he enjoyed it.

Four years later, Alfred and Mabel Emily Spasshatt were married (in April 1890) in Armidale and after honeymooning in New Zealand they settled in a house which Henry had built for them in Thalgarrah's East Paddock they called Swallowfield (and which we are calling Swallowfield NSW.)

22. *His grandson, Keith Bigg, on the strength of this association, also spent some mid-terms in 1939-40 at this wonderful old house, run in traditional English style complete with butler and servants to wait at table. Tom Barker would meet him at Narellan railway station and drive home in an 1898 Delarge car, or their more modern 1902 vehicle.*

23. *See Annex B for details of the "Clyde".*

Alfred and Mabel's six children were all born at Swallowfield NSW over the next 13 years-

Ethel Mabel	-born 13.1.1892 (known as Essie)
Edward Lionel	-born 16.11 1894 (known as Lionel)
Henry Percival Sicard	-born 4.12.1896 (known as Percy)
William Spasshatt	-born 15.4. 1901 (known as Bill)
Audrey Frances	-born 30.9.1903
and Frederick John	-born 29.6.1905 (known as John Frederick, for some reason.)

There was a period of severe drought in 1902, the year when Henry Bigg died at Thalgarrah. As a result of the lack of rain the lake dried up, and it was necessary to dig a well on the flat ground north of the lake where an underground stream was found. Here a windmill was erected to pump water to the house. A high tankstand with two tanks at the back of the house was put in and this arrangement provided the main water supply until the 1930s. (The underground stream still provides the water to the present day, but electric pumps now do the job of the old windmill.)

By 1906 Mabel was suffering signs of paralysis in her arm and leg after a fall from her horse some three years earlier. As she had a young family and was a talented pianist and needlewoman, this was a great worry. The doctors didn't seem to have an answer, so the decision was made that she should go to London for specialist treatment. They left the three youngest children behind in Armidale with Mabel's widowed mother (Angela Spasshatt) and sister Rosalie.

Alfred, Mabel and the three older children aged 15, 13 and 11 sailed for England in May 1907 on the "Moldavia".[24] Unfortunately, the children managed to catch measles on the ship and arrived at Swallowfield rather spotty, which didn't please Uncle Fred, but Aunt Rose made them all most welcome.

The two boys were enrolled at a boarding school at Haywards Heath in Sussex, so as to ensure that their education was not too disturbed, but no mention was made of Essie's schooling.

Alfred and Mabel did a tremendous amount of sightseeing in between seeing doctors and specialists in various parts of England and Scotland.

A cousin of Mabel's mother, Harriet Mary Moule nee Elliott, was the wife of the Bishop of Durham, the Revd. Handley Moule, and the following letter describes their visit to the Bishop and his wife at their home in Bishop Auckland:

Thursday night, 31st October 1907.

We left London by the 10 train, changed at York and Darlington and got out at Bishop Auckland, 10 miles from Durham. I was waiting by the hatbox and suitcases etc. and Alfred was seeing after the luggage when a grand footman in blue livery with gold buttons with a mitre on them (I saw the mitre afterwards, I was too flabbergasted at

24. *The "Moldavia" is also covered in Annex B.*

the time) came up and asked if I was for the castle. I felt inclined to say no but had to confess I was, so he took the bags and off we went to the carriage and we both got in. I devoutly hoped it would be a long drive but we got there in no time, drove through some big gates and up to a side entrance. Of course, where we ought to be very impressed and serious we both wanted to laugh. A butler opened the door and a footman was standing behind him. I tried to take off my big coat gracefully and dropped my muff, handbag and parasol, bang, bang, bang - then we went down miles of corridors to a nice cosy room where Cousin Mary was waiting by a fire. She is most kind and cordial and after talking for a while took us to our room, a great big one with a fire - then we went on and saw the reception rooms. A drawing room about 100 feet long, really!-simply huge- the banquet hall and staircase leading to it. Then on to the private chapel. A most quiet, sacred, lovely place. Then back to our room where we were to rest till teatime at half past four.

This had been the Bishop's residence for 900 years and we both felt too undignified and Australian to be staying here. For one thing the water they brought us to wash our hands was cold and Alfred wondered if we could find a billy to heat it in. Then he began quoting "Clancy's gone to Queensland droving and we don't know where he are"[sic] - and then wondered how much we must give all those Johnnies (as he called the butler, footman etc) before we could get out again.

Well, we found our way to the sitting room again and met a very nice boy, or rather, young man, called Elliott, a nephew of Cousin Mary's. Then we had tea, two other ladies were there and then the Bishop arrived. He seemed very kind. Then two other clergy and their wives came. We are to stay until Monday or Tuesday. But, goodness me, the house oppresses me. Alfred says he hopes the King won't ask us to stay with him! What is dinner going to be like to-night? I am glad I have my velvet dress...

Friday night

I am waiting until Alfred comes up to do up my dress, so I can add a little more. I was very glad of the velvet dress last night and hope I impressed the butler. I really must make him understand that I am not in the habit of dropping muffs, umbrellas etc. We all met in the state room, it has a throne at one end where the bishops sat when people were presented at court. A Mr Edison, one of the Chaplains, took me into dinner. I was not a bit nervous of him or the Bishop, it is the butler and footmen that scare me. Such a pretty table, all fairy lights and white nephretos roses and asparagus fern. I know you want to know what we had for dinner, the butler and the two footmen waiting. Soup of course, then some sort of fish souffle, then roast chicken and vegetables, then a cream blancmange and cheese wafers with cream on them and then finger glasses and dessert, huge grapes and pears and candied fruits. Afterwards, Mr Elliott sang in the huge drawing room. He has a lovely voice and at a quarter to ten we all went into the beautiful chapel for prayers. Such a treat, mother, the wonderful feeling of antiquity about it and the sweet organ echoing up in the lofty roof, we had "Sun of my soul". Then to bed. Alfred said he was sure the butler would not let him come to my room because his pyjamas were laid out in the dressing room and the bed had been turned down. However, we chanced it. But that man really haunts me. Do you know what happened this morning? I got up early because being All Saints Day there was an 8 o'clock celebration in the chapel. The bath was waiting but I wanted the sponge which was packed in one of Alfred's bags in the dressing room. So I went to get it, saying, just in joke "perhaps the butler might catch me". I had no sooner opened the door and had just got to the portmanteau when I heard someone at the outer door. I turned and ran but it was the butler coming to see to Alfred's clothes and he must have caught sight of my vanishing nightdress!!!

The rest of the visit was pleasant and without further trouble with the butler.

Sadly, the doctors' treatments did not get to the root of the trouble and Mabel remarks in her letters that writing was difficult for her, as it was her right arm that was worst affected.

On returning to Swallowfield NSW Alfred was kept busy with the management of Thalgarrah, and with building alterations to keep pace with his growing family. The dining room at Swallowfield was enlarged with a floor to ceiling window letting in so much more light, and a pantry added. Another bathroom was put in and the 30ft. passageway to the kitchen block was enclosed, but only on the western side. The kitchen was enlarged, a laundry, storeroom and another bedroom for kitchen staff added. The boys slept out "in the barracks", a three bedroom cottage at the back of the kitchen.

In 1908 Alfred bought a property near Curlewis and Mt Digby called "Digby". This was on the Liverpool Plains, some 225km to the south-west of Armidale. At the time Alfred's views on the venture were *"Good farming and hopefully it will pay for itself in a few years"*. He also believed Mabel would be warmer there in the winter months as she was by now starting to suffer from the cold. But Digby did not turn out to be a success. In 1909-10 rabbits poured across the countryside eating out the grass, following which thistles of all descriptions germinated and took over. At the age of 18 the oldest boy, Lionel, left school (The Kings School, Parramatta) and tried to manage Digby, but the situation by then was beyond recovery. Farming wheat and oats did pay, but not sheep. Lanes had to be cut through the thistles for the sheep to get to water and the poor dogs had to wear heavy leather "shoes". Digby was sold at a loss in 1916.

In 1911 Alfred's mother Annie had died and left Thalgarrah vacant. The decision was taken by Alfred and Mabel to move in to Thalgarrah, but before this could happen alterations had again to be made to accommodate the whole family and their needs. Mabel was in a wheelchair and she had a companion, a Miss Ellaby (then later a Miss Hole) and there were extra staff. The children were by no means convinced that the move to Thalgarrah was a good thing, and much resistance was put up along the way.

The amount of work involved in moving the family to Thalgarrah was considerable, and took nearly two years. Alterations were carried out in 1912 when a larger stable with feed room and a storage loft were added. A lean-to was put up on the southern side to house the family car, an Oakland, which in due course became affectionately known as "Old Bones". Barracks to house the boys (the farm hands) transferring to Thalgarrah were going to be needed and the decision was taken to move the barrack block from Swallowfield NSW in one piece. This proved quite a feat and at one point there was nearly a disaster. As the building was being drawn over the low river bridge it suddenly swung sideways and was in danger of toppling over into the river. The horses were quickly unharnessed and every hand and shoulder had to be applied to manhandle it back on to the sled, in proper alignment. Eventually the barracks were safely emplaced between the tennis court and the house at Thalgarrah, where they stayed until (about)1960.

Whilst all this upheaval and preparation work was going on between 1911 and 1913, there was another major event being planned - a wedding. On 2nd April 1913 Alfred and Mabel's eldest daughter Ethel (Essie), then 21 years old, married Phillip Arundell Wright. The wedding was held at Thalgarrah church, and the reception in a marquee on the lawn at Swallowfield NSW. Young Bill, aged 11 got fed up with the wedding hoo-ha and went to the lagoon to catch fish, frogs and yabbies. But as boys do when they go fishing in muddy lakes he got his clothes wet and was in lots of trouble when finally he went home. After all, they were his best clothes!

Alfred, Mabel and their family eventually moved out of Swallowfield NSW and into Thalgarrah at the end of 1913. Within a year, however, the Great War had broken out in Europe. Lionel, who had been working at Thalgarrah and at Digby, at the age of 18 enlisted in the AIF and in September set sail for overseas duty.[25] His brother Percy, two years his junior, enlisted in July 1915. Various relations lived at Swallowfield NSW until Harold (Tad) Curtis married Grace Smith in January 1918 and moved in there while their new home was being built on the Brooklyn property, a little closer to the Rockvale Road than the Brooklyn homestead.

Lionel returned from service overseas at the end of WW1 and married Hazel Lee from Bathurst in March 1919. To accommodate them Swallowfield NSW was extended and renovated. A bedroom, bathroom with a chip heater, and septic system were added on the north-west side of the house. They had two children, Nancy and Keith, both being born at Swallowfield NSW.

Mabel's condition deteriorated and by 1918 she could just manage to feed herself. She would read to her grandchildren, but they had to turn the pages for her. She died in 1925.

Before her death, however, two events concerning Swallowfield NSW have to be recorded. First, in 1921, closer settlement on the land for returned soldiers was a strong ideal with the then Government. Thalgarrah was large enough to come under the Closer Settlement Act, so Alfred Bigg sold the East Paddock to the Soldier Settlement Commission, who in turn sold it to his son Lionel. So the house and block was merged with and became known as Swallowfield, though it continued to be run as part of Thalgarrah for many years. Secondly, in 1922 Alfred had returned to England following the death of Aunt Fanny (Bigg). The Hyde was going to be sold and he had been afforded the opportunity to choose the furniture, silver etc that he wanted. The wonderfully carved chests and other items dating from around 1600-1630 were divided between the Bigg and Curtis families.

(On this trip Alfred took his youngest daughter Audrey, then aged 19, with him. Before leaving he had instructions from Mabel that he was not to let Audrey become entangled

25. *Lionel was one of the first to enlist in the 1st Australian Light Horse. His Army number was 512*

with any young man, especially not a shipboard romance. However, Alfred failed to carry out his commission from Mabel!)

After Mabel's death Alfred continued to live on at Thalgarrah, helped by a succession of housekeepers, but with the Depression restricting any large expenditure. His son John also lived there with his wife (Brenda Wilshire) in a part of the house converted into a flat, and for a time after they were married another son Bill and his wife (Mary Bowman) also lived there

When war came for the second time, in 1939, Bill, Lionel and John joined the Armed Services, and John and Bill's families moved for a time to Sydney. Les and Alice Gurd moved over from Swallowfield NSW to housekeep for Alfred, and Les, with Lionel's daughter Nan, took over the running of the property with Alfred's experience to help them. Lionel managed to get leave to return for shearing. Another series of housekeepers followed the departure of Les and Alice, but in 1942 Alfred suffered a slight stroke. He made a good recovery initially, with the help of a nurse, but he died at Thalgarrah the following year.

(It was mentioned in Chapter 3 Henry's Story that Alfred's birth was not registered in the conventional way, as he was born on the 6th December 1862 on a droving trip, as it were, somewhere between Rockhampton and Mount Morgan, and the birth was not registered until some two years later. All he ever had was his baptismal certificate. He was never registered at a Court House and thus does not (and never did) appear in the official records of births in Queensland. Alfred Bigg was probably 5 days short of his 81st birthday when he died, although his death certificate records him as "Male 81 years".)

Alfred was remembered in later life as a quiet, gentle man, quite stocky, standing about 5′10″, with a large bristly moustache stained with tobacco. He had snow-white hair from his mid-twenties, so always looked older than he was. In his early days he was a good rider and never seemed to be comfortable driving a car. However, he taught his grandchildren to drive in his model 1926 Ajax. He was a keen shot, a good trout fisherman and a wily tennis player and picnic days of fishing, duck shooting and kangaroo drives were his recreation. From these developed the giant annual Boxing Day picnics for all friends and relations under the trees planted by his father. He was a keen supporter of the Show Society and his church, taught his grandchildren to play crib, and was a good story-teller.

The family trees of Alfred and Mabel Bigg's four sons Edward Lionel, known as Lionel, Henry Percival Sicard, known as Percy, William Spasshatt, known as Bill and Frederick John known as John are given in Annex A.

Augusta Emily (born 1864)

As we have already heard, Amy had married her third cousin, Henry Welch Curtis, soon after he arrived from England to gain experience in farming in Australia. He had bought 12,000 acres bordering on Amy's parents' property. Approximately 500 acres of her parent's land, Thalgarrah, had been given to Amy and her new husband as a wedding gift, and they called their new home "Brooklyn".

They had three daughters and two sons-

Frederick Henry Bigg Curtis	born 28. 4.1889
Evelyn Augusta Bigg Curtis	born 27. 5.1890 (known as Eva)
Harold Bigg Curtis	born 17. 7.1891 (known as Tad)
Mary Bigg Curtis	born 27. 9.1892 (known as Molly)
Winifred Delmar Curtis	born 19.10.1903

Strangely both sons and two daughters were given forenames of Bigg, but the last-born daughter wasn't?

All the children were born at Brooklyn and educated in Armidale. Both the boys went to The Armidale School (TAS for short), whilst the girls went to The New England Girls' School (known as NEGS.) Incidentally, whilst Frederick got shortened to the customary Fred, Harold was less fortunate. As he was a comparatively tiny baby, and had once been affectionately described as being as small as a tadpole, he became known to family and friends as Tad!

Amy's husband, Henry Welch Curtis, enjoyed a gamble in line with being a natty dresser and a very good horseman. In due course he bought another property "Abbey Green", north of Brooklyn and east of the small town of Guyra, and installed his eldest son Fred to manage it, running cattle and merino sheep.

Fred made a success of this venture and bred high-quality Hereford stud livestock. In 1916, Fred married Helen Everett, daughter of a well-known New England pioneer, and they had three sons and a daughter. His grandmother Annie Bigg died at Abbey Green in 1911.

However, the two brothers, Fred and Tad, had many differences of opinion over their respective grazing properties. Although Fred had sheep at Abbey Green he was a cattle man, whereas Tad who remained at Brooklyn continued to run sheep. The problems centred round the fact that Fred never built a shearing shed on Abbey Green and sent his sheep from Abbey Green to Brooklyn every September/October for shearing. As labour was cheap, it was relatively easy for Fred's sheep to be driven across to Brooklyn and back after shearing, but it was Tad who had to find the feed for the extra animals and men. And when the weather turned cold or wet, or feed was scarce, Tad was burdened with additional problems.

After World War II, when Fred's eldest son Owen took over, the two businesses were finally separated which ended Tad's difficulty. Fred died in 1970, and Abbey Green was sold nine years later.

Henry Welch Curtis died in 1924, but Amy continued to live at Brooklyn with her youngest daughter Winifred, until they retired to Armidale in 1938. Amy died just two years later.

Tad continued to run Brooklyn, mainly running sheep, but his great love was horses. He was an accomplished rider and won many prizes at the local shows. When his mother moved away to live in Armidale, he moved in to Brooklyn with his wife Grace, leaving his old home (Gooyong) to their son Walter (Wally) to live in.

Grace died in 1973 and Tad survived alone at Brooklyn for another 9 years. With Tad's death Wally and his wife Nerida continued to run cattle on Brooklyn, but gradually sold various paddocks, until they sold the last blocks in 1998, retiring to live in Armidale.

The Brooklyn homestead gradually fell into disrepair, and was pulled down in the 1990s. Only a few bricks and some stone steps now mark the spot of the home that Amy and Henry Welch Curtis had built when they married some 100 years earlier, in 1888.

So this chapter ends the story of Brooklyn and Thalgarrah, two properties that were such a part of the life of the Bigg and Curtis families from the mid-1880s through to the 1980s. Although the house at Brooklyn has gone, Thalgarrah flourishes and still overlooks the lake that Henry Edward Bigg created - and the English trees he planted remain an outstanding feature of the landscape to this day.

But this leaves us to finish with news of Swallowfield NSW, once the home of Alfred and Mabel Bigg. Mabel had died in 1925, and Alfred 18 years later.

Alfred Edward Bigg, grandson of Smith Henry Bigg

Chapter 12
Swallowfield NSW

Alfred died in 1943 and when his sons Bill and John returned from serving in World War II the decision was taken to divide up the Thalgarrah and Swallowfield properties. Nancy recalls the method they adopted for deciding who should take what followed a good Australian tradition - they drew straws to see who would have first choice! Bill picked correctly and took the Thalgarrah homestead and paddocks to the north, Lionel came second and had Swallowfield and paddocks to the west, leaving John with the southern section on which he built a new house and outbuildings, which he called "Meraway". Two large outlying paddocks were sold to neighbours, to give everyone some ready capital.

In February (or March) of 1947 a new generator was installed to provide electricity at Swallowfield. That was the last improvement to the old property. On the night of the 26th May 1947, Nancy Bigg, Lionel's daughter then aged 27 was woken by an old pet sheep bleating. She discovered the kitchen block well alight and, as it was of wooden construction, the fire spread quickly. Even so, Nancy and her mother and father were able to remove some clothing, silver and furniture. In desperation Nancy and Lionel seized the big, heavy roll-topped desk that was so much prized and deposited it on the front lawn in what seemed like no time at all. When the new house was built it took a crane and three strong men to put it into its new position. The fire appeared to have started under the copper in the laundry, but just how or why was never discovered. Swallowfield NSW was destroyed, the family had lost a lot of possessions and personal effects, but fortunately no-one was injured - thanks to the bleating sheep.

Lionel Bigg and his family decided immediately that Swallowfield would not be abandoned, but would be rebuilt. Lionel had already built a new workman's cottage, so the family moved into that for the time being. Timber was cut by April the following year, mainly blackbutt and stringy bark from what was known as Peter's Paddock. This area also supplied timber for Meraway, alterations to Thalgarrah by Bill, and the shearing shed on Swallowfield.

The new Swallowfield was built to Lionel and Hazel's design, comfortable and easy to run, with open fireplaces, an Aga stove, an updated water supply from the mill and pump on the river. The builders were Bill and Dave Blanchard, a father and son combination. George Swan and George Charlton did the painting and Jack Burton the brickwork, steps etc. Lionel and Keith Bigg (and anyone else who could contribute their time) helped in general labouring. The Bigg family moved into the rebuilt homestead on 13th/14th April 1948.

The next serious and tragic event affecting Swallowfield occurred one day in November 1959. The mailman passing on his rounds didn't usually call in, but by chance he did that day. He found that there had been an explosion in the kitchen involving the kerosene fridge. Unfortunately, Hazel must have been close at hand when it happened, and had taken the full force of the blast. There was no-one to help at the time, so the mailman's visit was fortuitous. Hazel was rushed to hospital, but her injuries were severe and she died on 29th November. The fire didn't take hold, thankfully, so the house wasn't burnt down for a second time; the walls were just badly scorched.

Lionel remarried after this tragic incident and his new wife was Eleanor (Nell) Wyndham. After they were married, on 17th December 1960, they continued to live at Swallowfield until Lionel died in 1969, aged 74.

After Lionel passed away, Nell didn't want to continue living at Swallowfield and Lionel and Hazel's two children, Keith and Nancy, were not in a position to take over the property and run it properly. Keith was working for CSIRO in Sydney, and Nancy was living with her family at Mackay, Queensland. So, reluctantly, the decision was taken to sell Swallowfield. The purchasers were their good friends John and Jean Adams, who were at that time running a large timber and plantation business in New Guinea, but looking to sell up and return home to Australia. Keith's wife (Robin) had been at school with Jean Adams. It didn't take long for the deal to be struck and in 1971 Swallowfield finally passed out of the hands of the Bigg family, and the Adams family took up residence in their new home.

Nancy comments that it was the best thing they could have done for Swallowfield; John and Jean Adams took good care of the property and developed it, putting in place the improvements that Lionel had himself dreamed of doing. The four Adams children grew up and married in the district. The Biggs and Adams families remain good friends. John Adams, now a widower, still runs Swallowfield.

Swallowfield NSW around 1910.

Swallowfield NSW around 1930.

Ian Waite surveys his splendid new home. *Photo - Tony Turner*

Chapter Thirteen
Epilogue

Our story has taken us over many years and has traversed the globe. It started in 1845 in Mannings Heath, West Sussex, England and finishes in Armidale, New South Wales, Australia some hundred and fifty five years later. But of course the story hasn't ended for good, it has just paused for a while. Time continues to flow and new generations of the Bigg line, descendants of Smith Henry Bigg and Augusta, through their son Henry Bigg, continue to thrive in Australia. And the properties we have seen mentioned are still all known by the names given to them by the Bigg and Curtis families.

In Mannings Heath, Swallowfield is now in magnificent order thanks to all the work of Ian Waite and his wife Lorely and family, although work will no doubt be continuing on Ian's various schemes for many years to come.

Swallowfield, late summer 2000.
The Waite family finally moved in to Swallowfield in December 2000. *Photo - Tony Turner*

The Church of the Good Shepherd, Mannings Heath built by Augusta Bigg in memory of her beloved brother William, and graced by the beautiful stained glass windows is still a treasured part of the community.
Photo - Tony Turner

St. Andrew's Church, Nuthurst remains a glorious picture, providing perpetual sanctuary to so many members of the Bigg family.
Photo - *Tony Turner*

St. Andrew's Church in Springtime. *Photo - Tony Turner*

At Handcross, a few miles from Swallowfield, The Hyde estate is still exceptionally beautiful. The East Wing was placed on the market in March 2001 at an asking price of £1,15M. *Photo - Tony Turner*

The lakes at The Hyde remain as picturesque as ever. *Photo - Tony Turner*

In New South Wales, Thalgarrah is still in good condition, overlooking Henry's pride and joy, his Sanctuary, the English woodland he planted - The author being introduced to Thalgarrah in February 2000 by (from left to right) Judith Fitz-Henry, Caroline Mitchell and Nancy McLean). *Photo - Tony Turner*

The lake and the English trees planted by Henry Edward Bigg viewed from Thalgarrah. *Photo - Tony Turner*

The rebuilt Swallowfield NSW in 2000, situated on the same ground as the original home that was burnt down in May 1947, provides a comfortable home for John Adams. *Photo - Tony Turner*

Thalgarrah Church, on the edge of the Thalgarrah Station, is still providing a service to the local inhabitants, and bearing witness to the Bigg family history. Thalgarrah in the background to the left

Photo - Tony Turner

Interior of All Saint's Church, Thalgarrah. *Photo - Tony Turner*

The windmill at Swallowfield NSW. *Photo - Tony Turner*

And the beautiful lagoon at Swallowfield NSW still has its fish, frogs and yabbies. *Photo - Tony Turner*

Annex A
Genealogy

Family trees have been included in Chapter 1 for EDWARD and SARAH BIGG and their children, and Chapter 2 for SMITH HENRY and AUGUSTA BIGG and their offspring.

Of Smith Henry and Augusta Bigg's five children no trees are needed for two of their children, Augusta and William, as they did not marry. The children of Edward Francis Bigg and his wife Fanny all died at an early age, before reaching adulthood, so no tree is necessary in their case, either. And although Frederick did marry (Rose Curtis), their marriage produced no offspring. Consequently a family tree is needed only for **Henry Edward Bigg.**

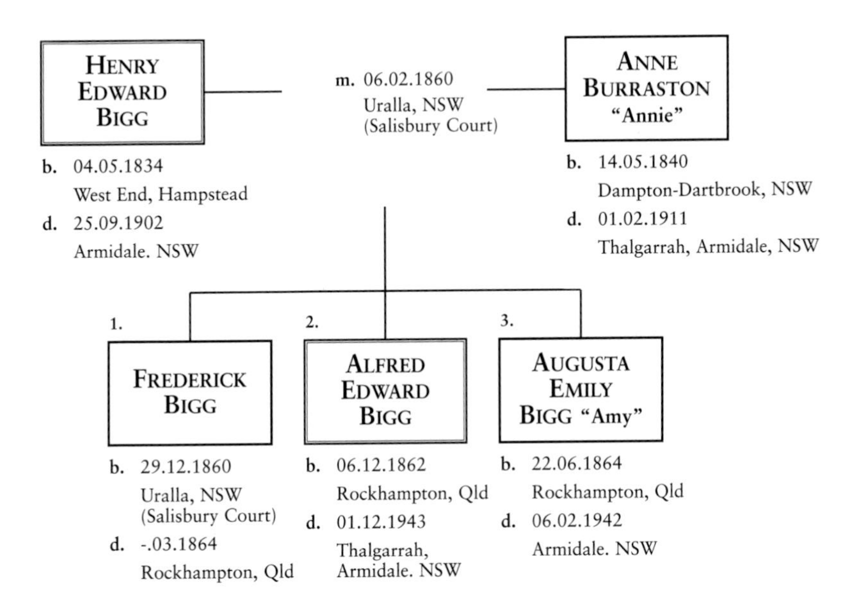

Chart 1

Following the male line, the family tree of **Alfred Edward Bigg** is as follows:-

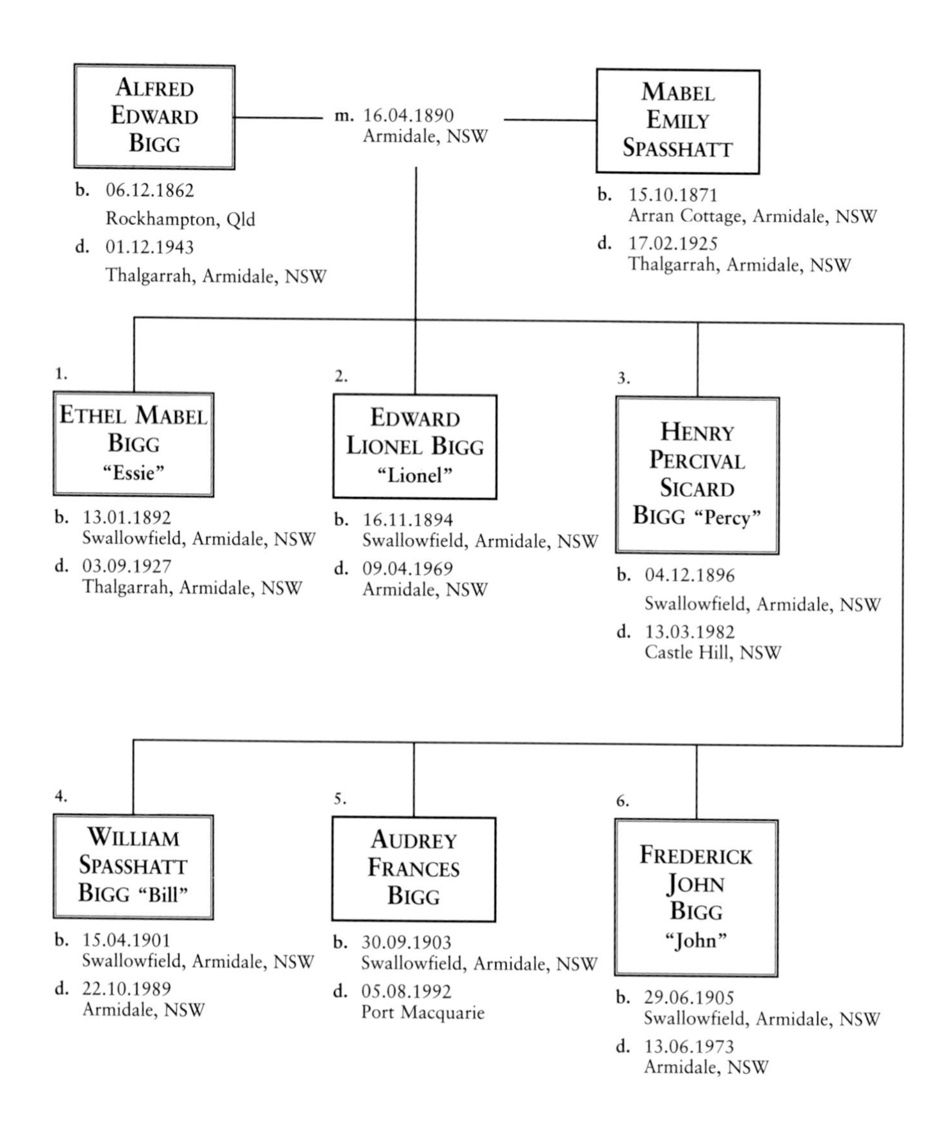

Chart 2

Following the male line again, family trees are necessary for the four Bigg sons, **Edward Lionel (Lionel), Henry Percival Sicard (Percy), William Spasshatt (Bill) and Frederick John (John).**

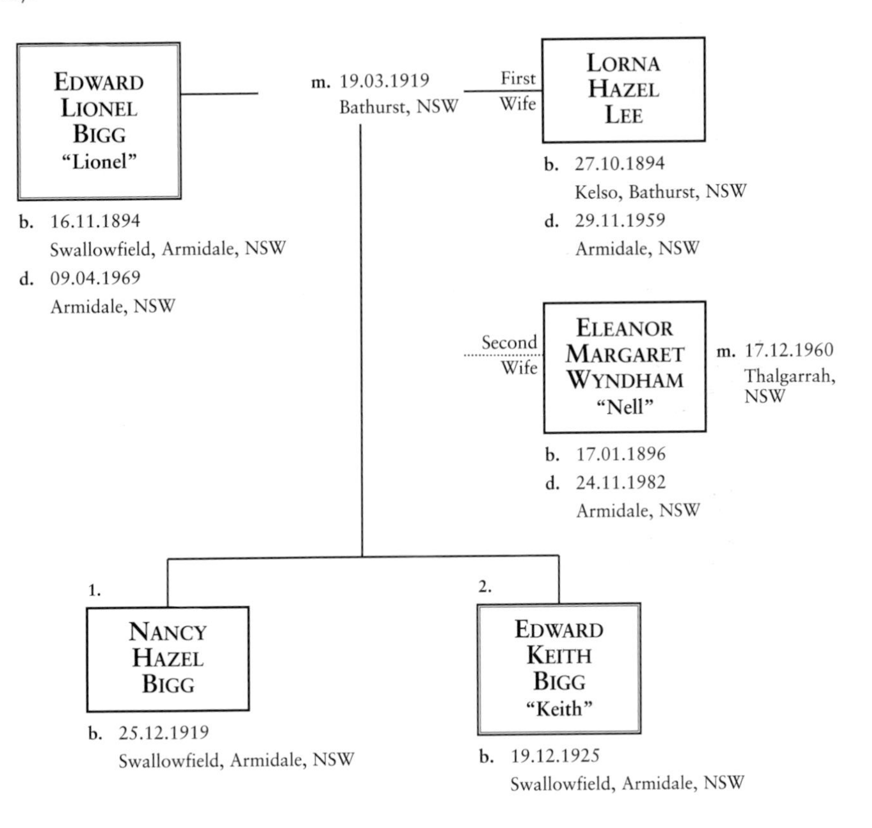

Chart 3

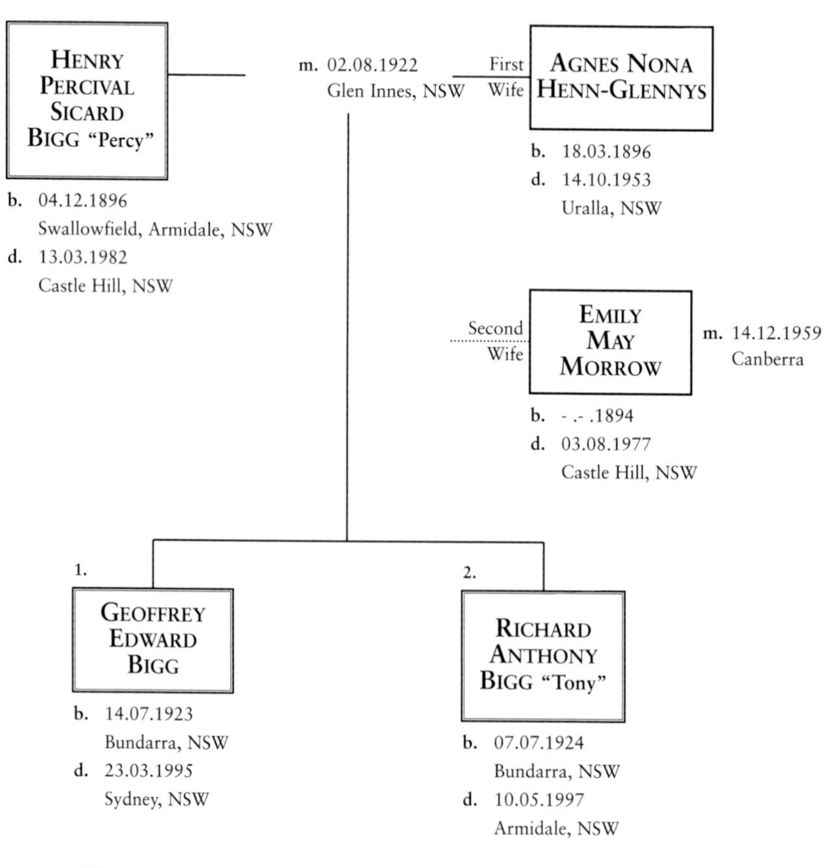
HENRY PERCIVAL SICARD BIGG "Percy"
b. 04.12.1896
Swallowfield, Armidale, NSW
d. 13.03.1982
Castle Hill, NSW
m. 02.08.1922
Glen Innes, NSW
First Wife
AGNES NONA HENN-GLENNYS
b. 18.03.1896
d. 14.10.1953
Uralla, NSW
Second Wife
EMILY MAY MORROW
m. 14.12.1959
Canberra
b. - .- .1894
d. 03.08.1977
Castle Hill, NSW
1.
GEOFFREY EDWARD BIGG
b. 14.07.1923
Bundarra, NSW
d. 23.03.1995
Sydney, NSW
2.
RICHARD ANTHONY BIGG "Tony"
b. 07.07.1924
Bundarra, NSW
d. 10.05.1997
Armidale, NSW
(NB. Percy's wives were sisters)

Chart 4

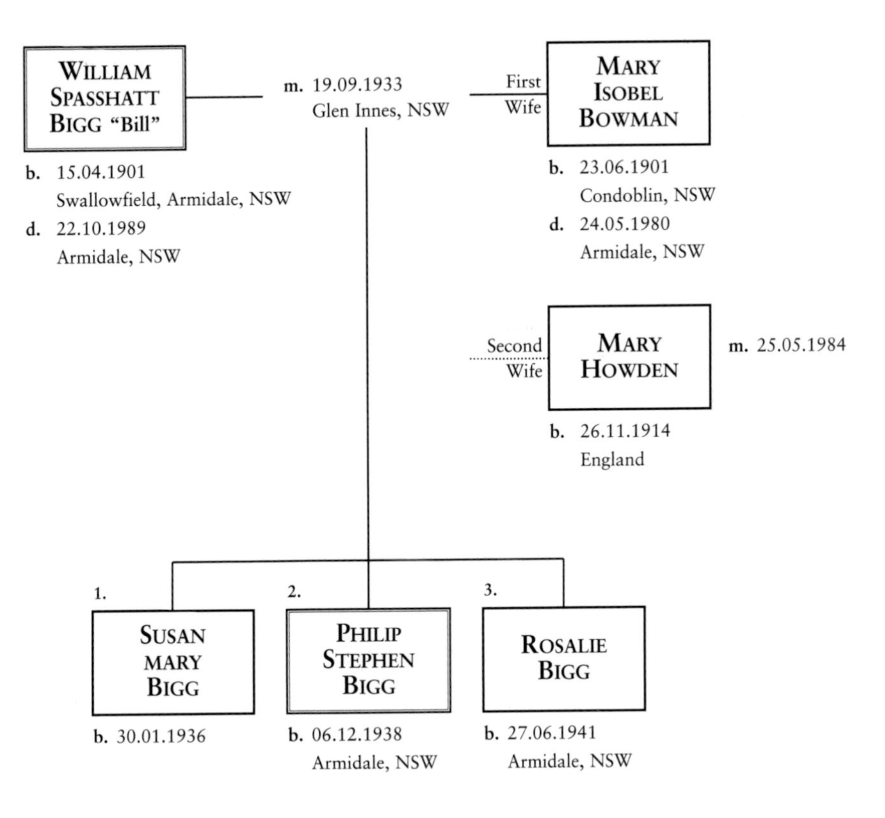
WILLIAM SPASSHATT BIGG "Bill"
m. 19.09.1933
Glen Innes, NSW
First Wife
MARY ISOBEL BOWMAN
b. 15.04.1901
Swallowfield, Armidale, NSW
d. 22.10.1989
Armidale, NSW
b. 23.06.1901
Condoblin, NSW
d. 24.05.1980
Armidale, NSW
Second Wife
MARY HOWDEN
m. 25.05.1984
b. 26.11.1914
England
1.
SUSAN MARY BIGG
b. 30.01.1936
2.
PHILIP STEPHEN BIGG
b. 06.12.1938
Armidale, NSW
3.
ROSALIE BIGG
b. 27.06.1941
Armidale, NSW

Chart 5

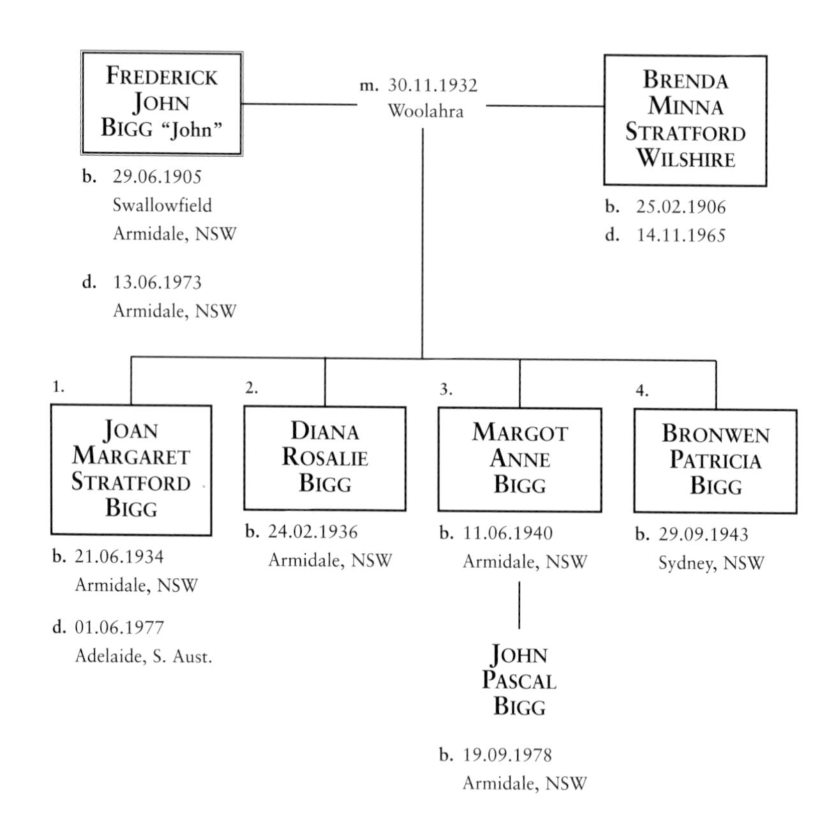
FREDERICK JOHN BIGG "John"
b. 29.06.1905
Swallowfield
Armidale, NSW
d. 13.06.1973
Armidale, NSW
m. 30.11.1932
Woolahra
BRENDA MINNA STRATFORD WILSHIRE
b. 25.02.1906
d. 14.11.1965
1.
JOAN MARGARET STRATFORD BIGG
b. 21.06.1934
Armidale, NSW
d. 01.06.1977
Adelaide, S. Aust.
2.
DIANA ROSALIE BIGG
b. 24.02.1936
Armidale, NSW
3.
MARGOT ANNE BIGG
b. 11.06.1940
Armidale, NSW
JOHN PASCAL BIGG
b. 19.09.1978
Armidale, NSW
4.
BRONWEN PATRICIA BIGG
b. 29.09.1943
Sydney, NSW

Chart 6

Continuing the male lines through the next generation, we find-

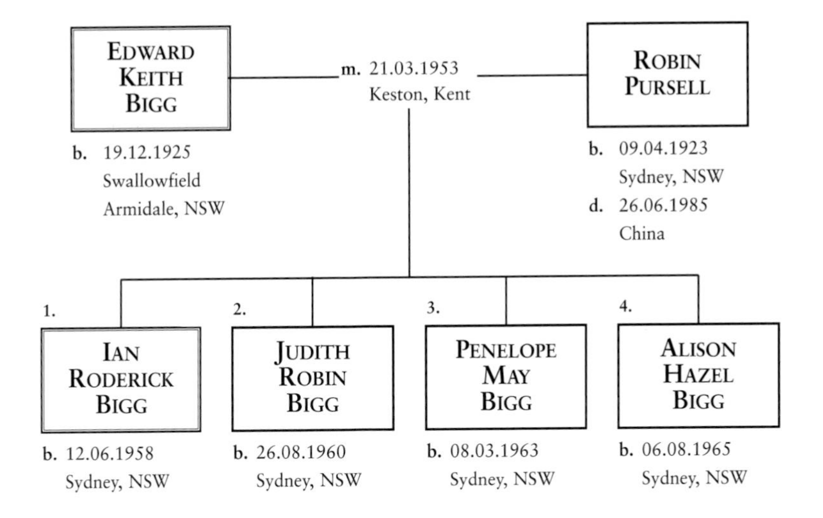

Chart 7

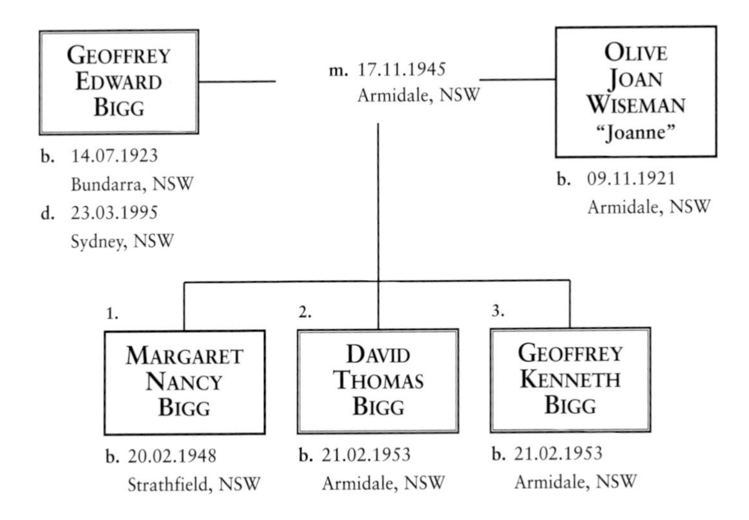

Chart 8

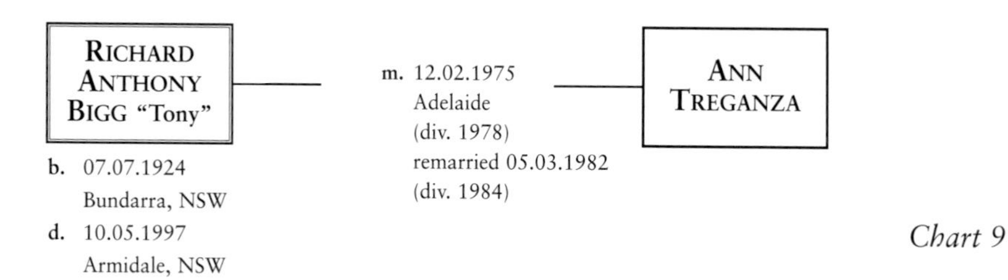

Chart 9

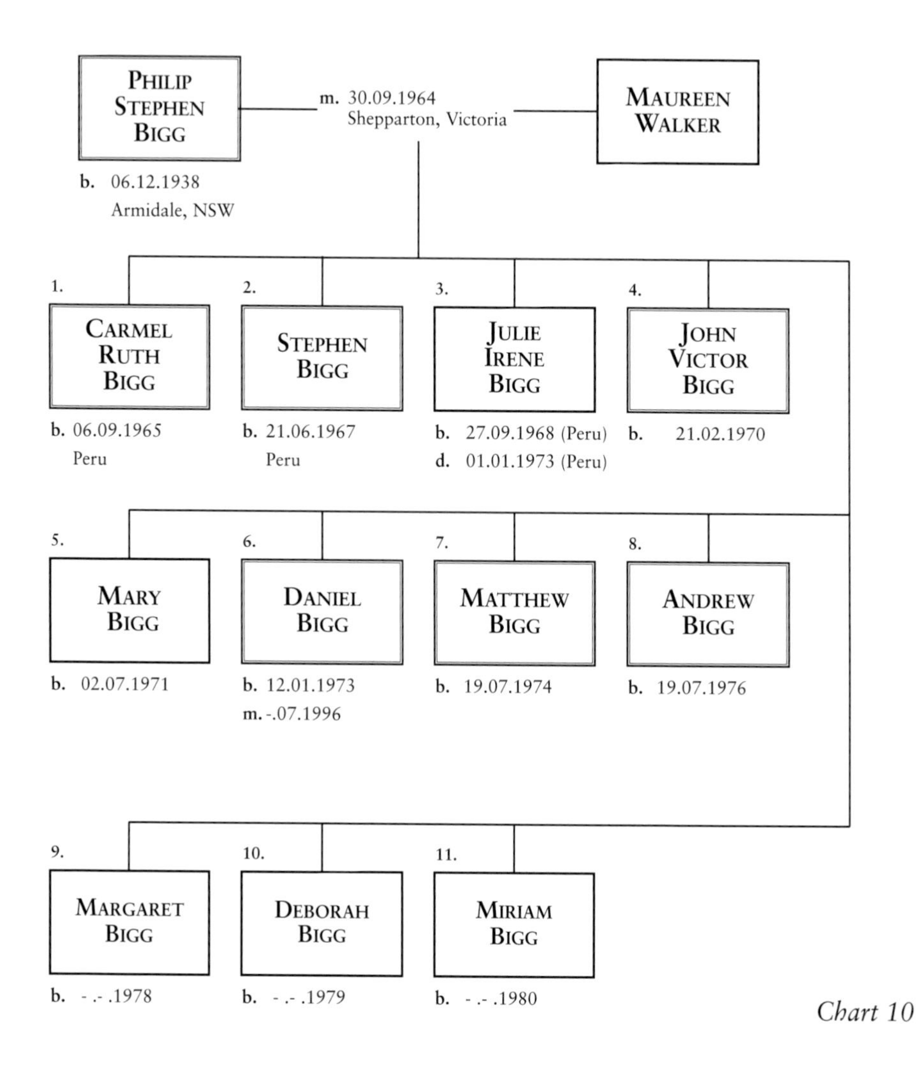

Chart 10

And so to another generation of Henry Bigg's descendants-

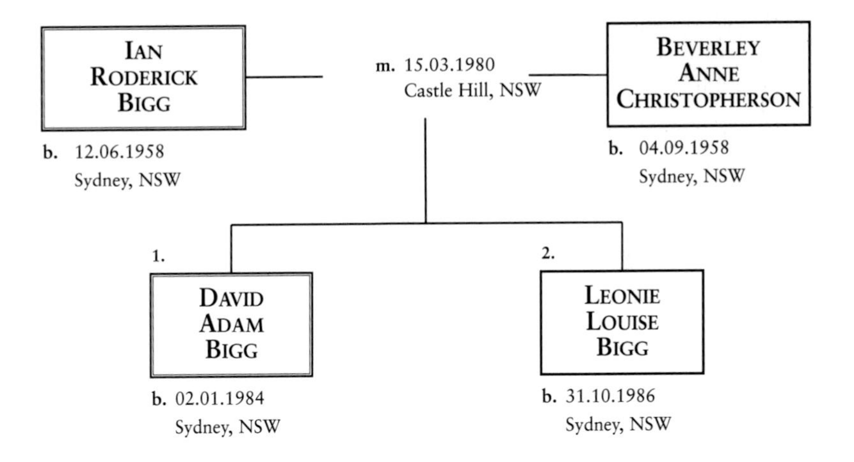

Chart 11

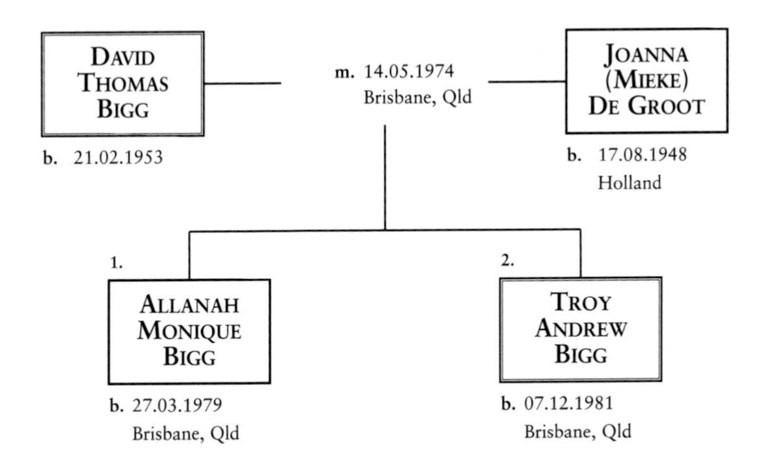

Chart 12

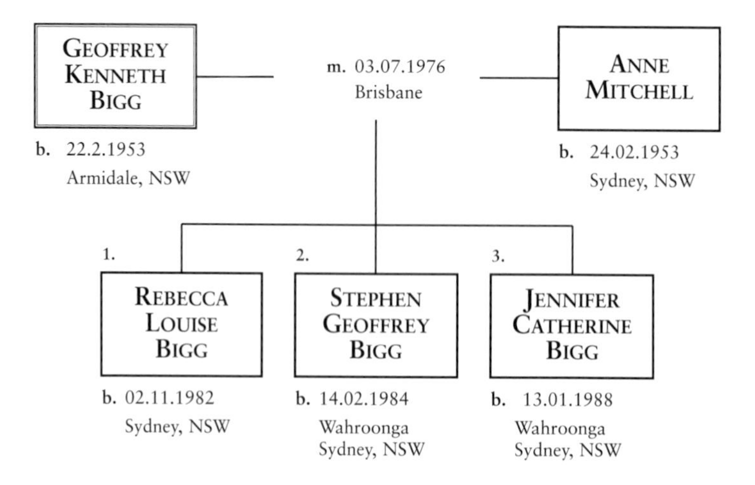
GEOFFREY KENNETH BIGG
m. 03.07.1976
Brisbane
ANNE MITCHELL
b. 22.2.1953
Armidale, NSW
b. 24.02.1953
Sydney, NSW
1.
2.
3.
REBECCA LOUISE BIGG
STEPHEN GEOFFREY BIGG
JENNIFER CATHERINE BIGG
b. 02.11.1982
Sydney, NSW
b. 14.02.1984
Wahroonga
Sydney, NSW
b. 13.01.1988
Wahroonga
Sydney, NSW

Chart 13

Annex B
The Vessels

Three vessels are mentioned in this book, apart from the "Maid Judah" which carried the "box" from England to Henry and his family in Australia in 1872 and other years.

The three ships were:-

- **Durham,** the vessel that Henry Bigg and his family took back to Melbourne from Gravesend in January 1877. (Chapter 3.)

- **Clyde,** on which Alfred sailed from Australia on the 27th May 1885 to start his "Gentleman's Grand Tour". (Chapter 11.)

and

- **Moldavia,** which carried Alfred and Mabel Bigg and 3 of their children to England in May 1907. (Chapter 11.)

Thanks to the National Maritime Museum, Greenwich, and Southampton City Council's Library, Archives and Information Services Department some information on these vessels is given overleaf.

Durham

Durham was an iron sailing ship of very nearly 2,000 tons, built in 1874 for the Australian shipping line of Money, Wigram & Co. Ships of their fleet were named after English counties. Durham was registered in the port of Liverpool. She was classed as an "ex-auxiliary steamer" in Lloyd's Register of 1887-1888, with her Master being W. Butler.

Vessels were taking the Cape route outward from Britain and returning via the Suez Canal in these times.

A good run for the time would be to make Melbourne in 44 days (the Kent made this run and the Somersetshire took from 45 to 50 days.)

Photo: National Maritime Museum, London.

Clyde

The Clyde was a three-masted, steel hulled, compound-engined schooner built in 1881 for P & O by William Denny. She was the only one of a fleet of five vessels ordered from Denny in June 1880 by P & O, the other orders going to Barrow Shipbuilders (two ships, Ganges and Sutlej), Harland and Wolff (one ship, Shannon), and J & G Thomson (one ship, Thames).

RMS Clyde was built at a cost of £114,900, which produced a loss of £35 for the yard, largely due to a labour strike in September 1880.

Powered by an 800 bhp compound engine driving a four-bladed steel screw, she carried 123 first-class passengers and 48 second-class. She was a vessel of 4099 tons.

She featured one of the earliest examples of architect-designed interiors for ships, with the fittings of the saloon and music room to designs by J.J.Burnett.

After operating on the Australian route for some years, Clyde was sold off to Borah of Bombay in 1901 (where she was renamed Shah Noor), and finally broken up in 1905.

Photo: National Maritime Museum, London.

Moldavia

At the turn of the century, P & O commissioned the construction of a fleet of large new passenger liners to be used on the Australian trade, calling them the "M" class - they would all be given names beginning with the initial "M". These new vessels would be the first P & O ships on the run to Australia to feature two propellers and could steam at 16.5 knots.

Built by Caird & Co at Greenock they were based on the highly successful fleet of five ships that P & O had built between 1896 and 1900.

The first ship of the class was the Moldavia, built at a cost of £336,178; she was handed over to P & O in August 1903. After a short cruise down the Channel with distinguished guests aboard, she made her maiden commercial voyage to Bombay and back.

Moldavia left Tilbury on her first voyage to Australia on 5th February 1904. (She was barely three years old when the Bigg family sailed on her to England.)

Moldavia provided accommodation for 348 first-class and 166 second-class passengers. She and her sister ship gave excellent service to P & O, who in due course built a further eight vessels of the M class, although these were to be slightly larger than the first pair.

In 1907, the same year that the Bigg family travelled on her to England (was it the very same voyage, perhaps?) Moldavia ran herself aground on the treacherous Goodwin Sands in the Straits of Dover. She was extremely fortunate in one sense, however, as she ran aground at low tide and was therefore able to float herself off as the tide rose.

Moldavia stayed on the Australian route (which included New Zealand from 1910) when the First World War broke out, but inevitably she was requisitioned and converted into an Armed Merchant Cruiser. Finally, she was bought outright by the Admiralty. In June 1917 her fine sister ship Mongolia fell to a mine laid by the German commerce raider "Wolf" off Bombay and was sunk with the loss of 23 souls.

Less than 12 months later it was the turn of Moldavia to be attacked. She was ferrying a full complement of US soldiers across the North Atlantic to Europe and was running up the English Channel to Beachy Head, with an escort, at the end of her voyage when she was torpedoed on 23rd May 1918 by German submarine UB57.

Following the torpedo strike she kept steaming for 15 minutes, but when it became obvious that she could not be saved, the boats were lowered away. An explosion killed 56 men, but the remaining survivors of the sinking were able to get away in boats to be picked up by escorting destroyers.

So ended the career of a splendidly styled M class liner.

Acknowledgements

I can own to discovering very little original material for this book; virtually all of it has been generated by others, and it has been my pleasure to unearth it and to bring it all together.

I owe an enormous debt of gratitude to all contributors, whether they provided documents, photographs, or agreed to submit themselves to video interviews. I hope I have remembered all of them here, but apologies if my memory has let me down to any I might have overlooked.

(in alphabetical order)

Augusta Bigg, for those wonderful diaries that made this book possible.

Dr Keith Bigg, for much material and ongoing help. Keith "translated" Augusta's longhand diaries which formed the basis of the chapter on 1845. He unselfishly loaned me his History of the Bigg Family, from which I have taken large extracts.

Nancy McLean, for providing lots of material, but most of all for the notes, the anecdotes and the guided tour of Swallowfield NSW and Thalgarrah in 2000.

Pat Curtis, her late husband Warwick, and daughter Corinne for lots and lots of information and for reading, checking and editing.

Camilla Douglas-Hiley, for her recollections of Swallowfield in the early 1980s.

The family of the late **Cecil Delmar Curtis** for much information and valuable photos.

Judith Fitz-Henry (great neice of Mabel Bigg nee Spasshatt) and husband John, another provider of valuable information and a proof reader par excellence.

Allen Flint, for allowing me to quote verbatim from his material on the Church of the Good Shepherd and life in Mannings Heath at the turn of the century.

Mary Habershon, for unstinting help with piecing together the story of The Hyde.

Gordon Jones, for providing such valuable information on Edward Smith Bigg and his connections with his practice and the fire insurance business.

Mary Long and her husband, for taking Hazel and me round St. Mary's Church, Slaugham.

Rob Middleton, for supplying information on the early railway situation in West Sussex.

National Maritime Museum Greenwhich, for permission to reproduce photographs of the Clyde and Durham.

Ordnance Survey, for kind permission to reproduce a map of part of West Sussex.

Southampton City Council, (City Library, Archives and Information Services) for tracking down information on The Maid of Judah, the Clyde, Durham and Moldavia.

Sussex Archaeological Society, Lewes, for kind permission to reproduce the print of St. Andrew's, Nuthurst from the Sharpe Collection.

Ian Waite, for his tireless patience and good humour in answering my endless rounds of questions, whilst he tried to re-build and re-furbish Swallowfield.

Finally, to my wife **Hazel** for her patience and understanding over the past three and a half years, whilst this book has been created.

Tony Turner